How to Make Cloth Books

for Children

**A Guide to
Making
Personalized
Books**

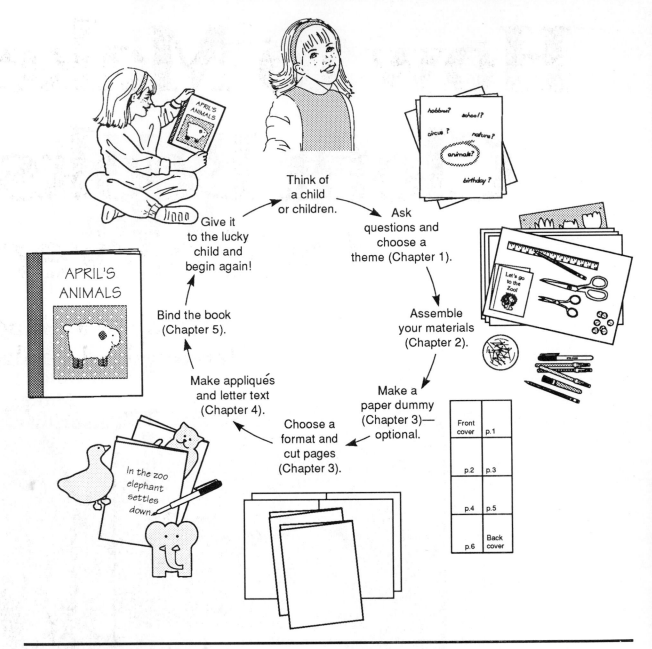

Think of
a child
or children.

Give it
to the lucky
child and
begin again!

Ask
questions and
choose a
theme (Chapter 1).

Bind the book
(Chapter 5).

APRIL'S
ANIMALS

Assemble
your materials
(Chapter 2).

Make appliqués
and letter text
(Chapter 4).

Make a
paper dummy
(Chapter 3)—
optional.

Choose a
format and
cut pages
(Chapter 3).

In the zoo
elephant
settles
down.

Front cover	p.1
p.2	p.3
p.4	p.5
p.6	Back cover

Other books by Anne Pellowski

Non-fiction

The Family Storytelling Handbook

Hidden Stories in Plants

Made to Measure; Children's Books in
  Developing Countries

The Story Vine

The World of Children's Literature

The World of Storytelling

The World of Storytelling, second edition

Fiction

Betsy's Up and Down Year

First Farm in the Valley

Have You Seen a Comet?

The Nine Crying Dolls

Stairstep Farm

Willow Wind Farm

Winding Valley Farm

How to Make
Cloth Books
for Children

A Guide to Making
Personalized Books

Anne Pellowski

Chilton Book Company
Radnor, Pennsylvania

Published in Radnor, PA, 19089, by Chilton
Book Company

Book design by Martha Vercoutere

Cover design by Rosalyn Carson

Cover photograph by Lee Lindeman

Interior photographs by Robbie Fanning

Illustrations by Pamela S. Poole

Edited by Robbie Fanning and Rosalie Cooke

Manufactured in Hong Kong.

Library of Congress Catalog
Card No: 92-54910

ISBN 0-8019-8398-3

1 2 3 4 5 6 7 8 9 0   1 0 9 8 7 6 5 4 3 2

iv

Foreword by Robbie Fanning, Series Editor

I come from a family of booklovers and uphold the tradition in my own family. When the three of us go on vacation, we take a change of clothes, freshly ground French roast (in case the coffee's pitiful), and a tower of books each.

Our daughter learned to read at an early age with handmade books my husband, Tony, drew and lettered for her. They incorporated scenes and objects meaningful to her: "Kali's Swim Story" and "Kali's Counting Book." He made them from cut-up manila folders, two holes punched in the fold, and tied with yarn.

We read commercial books to her, too, of course, but the personalized ones connected faster.

We were lucky. Our families read to us, we read to our daughter, and she will undoubtedly continue the chain when she has children. Not all are so fortunate. Something like 27 million Americans are functionally illiterate, unable to read directions, application forms, even birthday cards.

That's one of many reasons I'm proud to be associated with Anne Pellowski's *How to Make Cloth Books for Children*: its link to literacy. I've watched and heard the effect of these cloth books on people. Teachers immediately want to make one with their classes; parents want to make them for their children, scout group, church. Friends want to make them for new babies. In each case, it's an unselfish act for a child, one more way to share through reading.

I'd like to issue a quiet challenge. Once you've made a book or two, extend your cloth bookmaking skills beyond your friends and family. Call your local library to locate the literacy center in your town. Offer to work with a teacher/reader team. Talk to the person learning to read, about his or her family. Take notes on his or her words. Then make a simple cloth book tailored to that new reader's family that he or she can read to a child.

Let's use skills we may take for granted to spread the love of reading.

v

Table of Contents

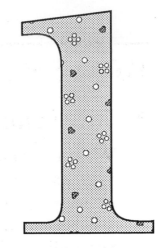

Introduction

Let's Go Fishing!

A book for Aaron
from Aunt Anne

One of two versions of the same book, this one for a grandnephew. All of the incidents and characters are based on Aaron's real life.

1

Introduction

✤ Why make cloth books? ✤ Who makes cloth books?
✤ How much time, how much money? ✤ Show off your books!
✤ Choosing a theme ✤ Questions to ask ✤ Making books for special children
✤ Some guidelines to consider in making books for *your* special children

2

*How to Make
Cloth Books*

For thousands of years, the passing on of values from one generation to the next has been done chiefly through stories. When the story is told by a parent or some other adult the child looks up to, and the telling is done in a compelling manner, the effect is lasting. The nuances of voice, the gestures, the often intimate ambiance of the setting where the telling takes place, and many other factors make the oral telling of a story a powerful and beautiful experience, often with life-long power.

Somehow, these same qualities must be made to come through in the stories we give to children in book form. If children are to appreciate the values in those stories, they must see in their outward format the same beauty and intimacy that they found in the spoken stories. And they should be able to find in their books the specific cultural content that they would find in the stories told in their families for generations.

For more than 25 years I have been fortunate enough to be invited to participate in many workshops, seminars, and conferences related to children's books, in many countries of the world. Often, I have been asked to give advice on methods for making attractive picture books, especially in areas where printing costs are high and good-quality paper must be imported at great cost. Of course, it is important to work for improvement in the quality of the printed books available to children in any given country. But I have always stressed the idea that instead of moaning about the lack of good books for children, one should do something about it.

In my view, the best way to start is by making handmade books that can be used with at least a small circle of children. This is especially true for areas of the world that are culturally heterogeneous, or where many languages are spoken in a small geographical area. It is unlikely, under present economic conditions, that such areas will have commercially produced children's books that will suit all the needs of the children.

In a number of workshops, I began to experiment with making books by hand. Usually, I selected a specific child or group of children for whom I made a book. Most of these first efforts were on paper. However, after a visit to Japan in 1978, where I saw some unusual cloth books being used with blind and physically handicapped children, it occurred to me that cloth was a much better medium than paper for making attractive books for children. It is often cheaper and more accessible in many countries. Also, it seemed so much more tactile and easier to manipulate. And cloth can give to the young child the soft feel of intimacy.

I began to make cloth books for children, and have been making several each year since that time. I made many mistakes in those first books.

However, with the availability of more and more new craft products, such as fusible webs and fabric crayons and pens, making the books began to get easier and they ended up being more attractive.

I started using these techniques in classes and workshops and found that many individuals and groups were stimulated to great creativity when working with cloth. Best of all, the child recipients loved the books, often because they could be personalized in special ways.

Marilyn Iarusso of the Office of Children's Services of the New York Public Library saw some of my cloth book creations. Working with a special grant from the Mayor's office, we were able to plan six workshops in literacy centers operating in various libraries of the New York system. To my great delight, the participants took to making cloth books with gusto and were able to express a wide range of creativity and personality. I have since repeated that workshop for other literacy programs, and for a number of schools, libraries, and other institutions or organizations.

These workshops were of necessity compressed, and virtually all participants asked for a handbook or manual that would contain more complete information. I began to describe some of my techniques in written form, and tried out various sections in workshops. *How to Make Cloth Books for Children* is the result. It is impossible to name the hundreds of persons who have participated in workshops, but my thanks are due to each and every one of them. Without them I could not have completed this book.

3

Chapter 1
Introduction

Fig. 1-1. This book was a joint project carried out by selected children in grades 5 and 6 at P.S. 155, Manhattan.

Fig. 1-2. *A Catfish Calhoun fabric print, this one of tropical fishes, was used to make a group book called* Under Tampa Bay. *This fabric was so attractive I bought yards and yards of it and used it for workshops in Venezuela, Egypt, Ghana, and Germany, as well as in many places throughout the U. S.*

Acknowledgments

Thanks to: Hiroshi Imamura of Kaiseisha Publishers, Tokyo, and the Coordinating Committee on Cloth Books for Children, for their inspiration; Billie Salter for locating many unusual patterned fabrics; Donna Salyers of Fabulous Furs, Covington, KY, for generous gifts of sample fake furs; Jane Genzel for permission to use photos from her handmade book; Isis Valeria Gomes of Brazil for permission to photograph *Au Au Lambau*; Marla Ostrowski for permission to photograph her handmade books; and to Brian Alderson of England, Hans Halbey of Germany, and Gina Abend of Random House Publishers, New York, for speedy and generous answers to my reference questions.

My thanks also to: Nina Reidarson of the IBBY Documentation Centre, Hosle, Norway; the staff of Central Children's Room, New York Public Library; reference staff at the Rare Book Division, Butler Library, Columbia University; Karen Nelson Hoyle of the Kerlan Collection, University of Minnesota Libraries; Ginny Moore Kruse of the Cooperative Children's Book Center, University of Wisconsin, Madison; staff of the Children's Literature Reference Department, Library of Congress; reference staff of the International Youth Library, Munich; Genevieve Patte and the staff of the Documentation Center, La Joie par les Livres, Paris; and to Doris Losey and all the participants at the workshop held in the Westgate Branch Library, Tampa, FL.

A special word of thanks to the many persons who wrote to tell me about cloth books they owned. Space does not permit me to list all of the names, but I wish to cite in particular: Mrs. Frieda Riggs and her daughter, Mrs. C. D. Spangler; Mrs. Doris Hall; Kathy Carlisle; Mrs. John J. Bucklin; Cynthis Dykhoff Garcia; Jenna Schulman; and Denise Waxman.

Finally, my deepest thanks to Robbie Fanning for the care and special attention she gave in bringing this book to completion.

Why make cloth books?

✤ **To keep as family heirlooms.** Many beautiful picture books are being printed for children today. A wide selection of these books is probably available in libraries and bookstores in your area. But each child and each family is unique. Each family experiences stories and situations in its own way. Making a book or two, in a long-lasting format like cloth, is a way of preserving that special family heritage. Cloth books can be passed on for generations.

✤ **To show your special ethnic or cultural background.** There are more than a hundred ethnic groups in the United States alone. It would be impossible for commercial publishers to cover all of the unique cultural traditions of each of these groups. In a handmade cloth book you can put in precisely the ethnic and cultural content you wish. This will help your child take pride in his or her heritage.

✤ **To help in the campaign for literacy.** Many persons who cannot read well are intimidated by writing, too. Having to write with pen or pencil on paper is often very hard for them. For many reasons, cloth seems to be a much more approachable medium. Discovering the ability to design, write, and put together a cloth book for a child or children, especially one with content taken directly from family situations and experiences, is very empowering.

✤ **To satisfy the desire for artistic expression.** Making books of cloth can bring out the fantasy, and the creativity, that lies hidden in all of us. You can explore a wide range of techniques.

✤ **To give children with special needs attractive, tactile books that are easy for them to handle, appreciate, and enjoy.**

✤ **For fun.** The best reason of all is the fun you can have sharing a handmade book with the child or children for whom it was made.

Who makes cloth books?

✤ **Groups.** It is exhilarating to create your books as part of a group working together. By sharing ideas, you can often come up with better results. Also, by pooling materials and equipment, you can reduce costs.

What kind of groups can make books together?

✤ Groups already functioning at a club, craft center, church, temple, senior citizen center, or similar environment.

✤ Classroom groups that have already made books in paper format in previous years and wish to try something new. (In my articles, talks, and workshops, I have expressed over and over again my belief that no primary-level teacher should be allowed to graduate from a teacher-training institution without first being required to design, write, and make a children's book.)

✤ Groups for new literates in libraries and other community centers.

✤ Parent education classes—it is important to involve parents, even those who know little of formal writing and reading, in the creation of books for their own children.

✤ Friends who get together informally for quilting or sewing.

✤ Families gathering for a reunion or special event.

✤ **Individuals.** I have made many cloth books on my own and have seen books by others, created all on their own. Even if you don't work in a group, it is usually a good idea to share the process and progress with family or friends; they can often suggest ideas or give just the right piece of material or equipment needed for your book.

How much time, how much money?

✤ Depending on the techniques selected, the number of pages, and the access to materials and equipment, it will take from 6 to 30 hours. For groups, this is best broken up into two to eight sessions of approximately 3 hours each.

✤ The cost of the materials will depend on the type of cloth selected and the techniques used. The materials for most of the examples shown in this manual ranged from $3 to $8 per book. This is less than the cost of the average printed book. Of course, this does not include the cost of your time.‘

Show off your books!

✤ If you are especially pleased with your results, you might wish to explore whether your local library will display your cloth books. Or perhaps your county or state fair will consider accepting cloth books for judging in a special category.

Choosing a theme

A theme unifies the book and makes it easier for you to decide on illustrations and text. A theme might be as simple as a counting or alphabet book. It might tell a well-known family story or describe a day in the life of the child.

Here are some of the ideas workshop participants have come up with while working on books for specific children:

✤ the daily routine of getting up, dressing, eating breakfast, going off to church or school, etc., but with clothing, food, activities very specific to that child;

✤ a story about the child's name, its meaning, and why this name was given to that particular child;

✤ a first book for a Hmong-American child, showing colors and patterns in toys and surroundings that are typical of Hmong tradition;

✤ birds that a little girl sees on walks with her grandmother in Central Park;

✤ a bilingual Hebrew and English book of baby's first words in each of those languages;

✤ a story about an immigrant grandfather and why he settled in Nebraska;

✤ the special activities leading up to a child's birthday, and a surprise at the party;

✤ unusual and imaginative descriptions of what a child wanted to be or could be when she grew up;

✤ the different aspects of life a child experiences while visiting two sets of grandparents, one in the U. S. and one in Central America, with emphasis on foods, plants, animals;

✤ a child's first trip to an unusual place, and the way she reacted to it;

✤ the things a child could look for, hidden in the natural environment;

✤ a book about the rain forest;

✤ a birth story, using swirls and swathes of cloth to indicate in an imaginative way the baby in the womb and out of it;

✤ a counting book of the fish and "treasures" hidden under Tampa Bay.

Questions to ask

You probably will be making your book for a specific child, or possibly for two or more children in the same family or in the same classroom. Select a theme by asking questions such as these:

1. *For what age child/children are you making your book?*

For ages 1 to 2, text and pictures should be large and should concentrate on only one or two details per page. Most of the ideas expressed should be very direct. Ambiguous or double meanings can be implied, as a second level to be appreciated by the adults who will read the book aloud to children, but these meanings should be subtle and not interfere with the directness and clarity that appeal so much to little children who are trying to make sense of their world. Just as they like

"Let's go fishing,"
said Aaron.
"We need worms,"
said Uncle Gary.
Aaron looked in the
flowerbed. He found
ants but no worms.

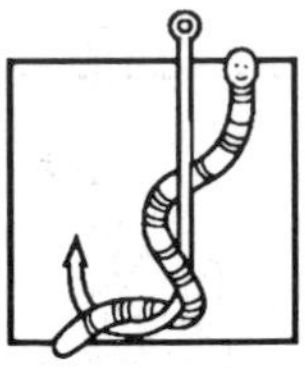

Fig. 1-3. *Each illustration in* Let's Go Fishing, *like this one, has insects or creatures (plastic) hidden behind flaps. Text can be read by new readers.*

the game of Peek-a-boo, children of this age like to lift flaps or open doors to find familiar or unexpected objects. (See *Marissa's Bedtime Book.*)

For ages 2 to 4, the same directness should be there, but increase the number of ideas or concepts on each page. The text, illustrations, and movable parts can be more complex, involving more response on the part of the child.

For age 5 or older, try to make the book *participatory.* Let the child move items, touch a variety of textures, find hidden objects. The text can be much longer, but should be printed in a consistent and clear style so that the child can easily read it herself or himself. (See *Let's Go Fishing*).

2. *Who are the family members for that particular child? What is special about their names, their occupations, their hobbies, their habits?*

Ellen is part of a big, extended family, each of whom likes to do many things. *The Flight of the Bumblebee,* made especially for her, allows the use of photos to be switched around, so that the family member hidden behind each flap must be guessed each time. The scenes accurately depict her family surroundings. April's father studied meteorology and passes on his interest in clouds. *Behind the Clouds* was created for her and her family.

3. *What are some of the things that you wish to call attention to in the child's environment?*

Many 2- and 3-year-olds are fascinated by bugs and insects. My sister Mary, my brother Francis, and my brother-in-law Roman are each avid gardeners. For several of their grandchildren, I created variants of a book showing the specific flowers each grows. Insects or bugs can be found hiding under flaps in each scene. (See *In Grandma's Garden* and *In Grandpa's Garden.*)

4. *What major family events do you wish to remember in some special way?*

Are there holiday customs, arrival-in-this-country stories, or birth stories that you wish to commemorate?

5. *Does the child's family have an ethnic background that you would like to celebrate?*

For example, *Charles' Story*, is for a young Chippewa, and *An Alphabet for an American Lassie*, is for a little girl who is half-Scottish.

6. *Are you trying to teach the child a few words in another language, perhaps the language of ancestors?*

Make a bilingual book. Stephanie and Paul were born in Korea, but have been adopted by my nephew and his wife. *The Korean-American Word Book* introduces a few Korean words for common objects found in their home.

7. *Do you want a group of children to take special note of things in a particular house or classroom?*

For the house of grandparents, or for a nursery classroom, you can make a participatory book that introduces the site in a particular way. By transferring slides to your cloth pages (see page 59), you can achieve recognizable scenes. *In Mrs. K's Classroom* introduces all the areas of Linda Kihslinger's kindergarten classroom at St. Monica's School. There are enough hidden "pockets" to enable her to put in photos of each of the children. This book can be used by several generations of students because the photos can be easily slipped out and substituted from the afternoon class or the following year's classes.

8. *What books has this child already enjoyed?*

Make a continuation of one of his or her personal favorites. For example, my grandnieces Rachel, Mia, and Heidi love the Spot books of Eric Hill (published by Putnam). However, when they go to visit their grandparents on a farm in Wisconsin, they see two other kinds of dogs, very different from Spot. This gave me the idea for *Spot Visits Willow Wind Farm*, their own personalized Spot book.

It is perfectly all right to get ideas from existing books and to adapt them to your

8

How to Make Cloth Books

Fig. 1-4. *Page from* Spot Visits Willow Wind Farm, *inspired by the Spot books of Eric Hill (published by Putnam).*

The Future of
Cloth and Tactile Picture Books

Co-ordinating Committee for the Promotion of Cloth Picture Books
Tokyo, Japan

Fig. 1-5. *Cover of the catalog and handbook describing the important exhibit of cloth books for children, held in Japan in 1978 and 1979.*

own personal use, as long as you do not intend to sell the books or use them for any commercial purposes. Of course, it is always a good idea to give credit to the author of the original. But you will probably get the most satisfaction from those ideas that you discover all by yourself, simply by observing the child or children for whom you are making the book.

A number of attractive cloth books are available commercially. Because of the hand work involved, most are quite expensive. Some currently available titles are listed on page 86. There are also patterns for cloth books in sewing pattern catalogs. However beautiful these are, many do not have the specific content that will match up with a given child and his or her family. If you can afford a commercially-made book, by all means get one. But consider also making another that fits exactly the interests and background of your child or children.

A few persons will make cloth books to order. Some of these are listed on page 85.

Making books for special children

It goes without saying that all children are special. Therefore, please read the following suggestions to help you plan the best book for your child.

"Special" children are those who, for one reason or another, need extra help in developing some or all of their learning skills. This could include blind or partially sighted or dyslexic children; deaf or hearing-impaired children; children with limited or no movement of one or more parts of the body; children with mental illness, retardation, or emotional imbalances; children who have grown up hearing and speaking a language in the home that is different from the language of the country or area in which they are living; children who have been given only restricted exposure to social and cultural interaction; or children who for no apparent reason have difficulty in learning to read.

It was a
red fox.
He ran
away
quickly.

Fig. 1-6. *Page from* What Animal Is That? *made for a grandnephew. The use of many textures in this book makes this appealing to partially sighted children.*

Ordinary reading demands much coordination of eye and brain. Often it involves the coordination of the hand and eye as well, as in holding the book at the proper angle, turning the page, etc. For blind persons, the hand substitutes almost totally for the eye.

Good coordination comes only with practice. The more practice the child gets in all forms of body and brain coordination, the better the chances that the child will learn reading more easily. For special children, starting from the time they are very young, it is easier to give practice in such coordination with cloth books, rather than with books of paper. Paper is harder to manipulate and tears quite easily when pulled or jerked. Also, cloth books are, as Hiroshi Imamura of Japan writes, "soft, warm, gentle and reassuring."

As mentioned earlier, *How to Make Cloth Books for Children* was stimulated in large measure by the extraordinary exhibition I saw many years ago in Japan, described in the booklet, *The Future of Cloth and Tactile Picture Books* (see Bibliography on page 81). While my goal is to help others create cloth books for *all* children, it is also my hope that in some small way this handbook can help to spread the concepts explored in that exhibition, namely:

1. That special children deserve to have beautiful and meaningful picture books that they can handle and enjoy in the same ways that so-called "normal" children enjoy picture books; and

2. That the handmade cloth book designed to respond to specific needs is probably the best introduction to books that can be given to special children.

Those who would like to make cloth books for special children from one or more of the categories listed above should begin by reading and looking at books already made for such children. Such books are rare, but they can usually be located by asking in children's departments of large public libraries, in state libraries, or in libraries in schools or institutions serving special children. Some of the more recent books can be located by using the list in "Books for Disabled Young

People," page 82. It is also possible to get a good idea of the types of books that have appeal for special children, by looking at the photos in the booklet *The Future of Cloth and Tactile Picture Books.* If your local library does not own that booklet, ask to get it on interlibrary loan.

But the best way to find out which kind of books appeal to *your* special child or children is to experiment by making some cloth books. By testing a few of them with special children you will probably learn more than any manual or textbook or expert can teach you.

Some guidelines to consider in making books for *your* special children

1. Find out as much as you can about the special physical limitations of the child or children for whom you wish to make books. If blindness is involved, for example, you will need to learn about the specific ways in which blind children are taught Braille reading, tactile picture and object reading, etc. For partially sighted children, you will need to know what minimum size of script and pictures they are able to perceive. For spastic children or other children who experience difficulty in physical control of the hand, arm, or eyes, you will need to know which motions are easiest, and which present a challenge. Therapists treating emotionally disturbed or mentally ill children will often want certain themes or subjects avoided or stressed. Children whose mental processes are slower than average usually need stories and pictures that are very consistent and that have an easy-to-follow narrative.

The children's specialist in your local or state library can usually direct you to good books and other information sources in your area. However, don't read or study so much that you become overwhelmed by all there is to know about such special children. This often results in too much emphasis on the "problem" aspects of these children's lives.

What you want to do is concentrate on the fun and pleasure you can bring to these children through the medium of cloth books.

2. Observe the specific child or children. Many of these children have the same interests as "normal" children of the same age. And just like most normal children, chances are they like pictures and stories about things that are familiar to them, but with an intriguing catch or twist to surprise them or make them laugh. They will also probably like books that include them as characters, especially books that retell some interesting event in their lives, or invent stories about their pets.

3. Choose carefully the colors and textures of any cloth you use. Find out if the child/children have trouble perceiving certain colors. Try to use as many textures as possible, but also try to match up the textures with the actual object being depicted. For example, if the background of a scene is a smooth, velvety lawn as in *Spot Visits Willow Wind Farm,* then use a piece of velvety fabric, not a scratchy one. If depicting pets or other animals, try to get bits and pieces of real or fake fur that closely resemble the animal described.

4. Virtually all children are curious. Hide things under flaps, but make sure the flaps are very, very securely attached to the page, and that they are large enough to allow for easy manipulation. You might wish to make them of triple thickness, if the fabric is light-weight. (See page 49.)

5. Select your script type and size very carefully. (See page 60.) If the child is already learning printed script in a special school, make sure you find out from the teacher which script is best. Be consistent and always make each individual letter in the same way. If the book is for a deaf child, you might wish to use sign language, as well as English.

6. If the child has difficulty dealing with most forms of verbal or written words, you might wish to investigate the system called Blissymbolics, a narrative form of printing that uses pictorial symbols. A number of children's books are printed with such symbols. They can be located in "Books for Disabled Young People." (See page 82.)

7. Use an easily identifiable object (such as a small plastic or cloth animal or human figure) that can be moved from page to page, thereby giving the child the feeling he or she is interacting with the characters in the story. Secure the object to the end of a strong string or cord and attach the string or cord to the corner edge of the front cover of the book. Have a pocket somewhere on the cover in which to keep the object. Use fastenings such as *Velcro*, zippers, buttons, and snaps only in cases where you are sure the child will not be frustrated by a physical inability to open and close the fastenings by herself or himself.

8. Find out if the child has a need for more stimulation or less stimulation to understand the meaning of words in their context. Some children like complex and detailed pictures, often with a riot of color. Other children need austere, calm images in medium primary colors in order for the message to get through.

9. Make sure that some emotion or feeling comes through, in both words and pictures. Concentrate on feelings such as love, joy, tenderness, humor, caring, and sharing. If you wish to deal with emotions such as anger, rage, or helplessness, be sure to get advice from a child psychologist or other person who has had a lot of experience helping children work through such emotions.

10. Most children like stories that end well. If you do wish to leave a book somewhat open-ended, make sure that the possible interpretations of the ending include some "happily ever after" choices.

Fig. 1-7. *A photo portrait was outlined on a transparency and then was enlarged by placing it on an overhead projector and projecting it onto the cloth page. The details were traced with a fade-away pen, then filled in with fabric paint. The whiskers were created with sandpaper.*

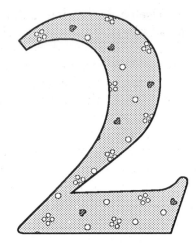

Organizing

Fabric collage book
inspired by workshops in
Kenya and Venezuela.

2

Organizing

❧ **Materials needed for a handmade cloth book**

❧ **Selecting a site**

You can certainly make a cloth book alone, but it's more fun to make one in a group. The instructions in this chapter are addressed to group leaders, but apply to you, too, if you're working alone.

If working with a group, agree on the number and frequency of sessions you will have, the place and time you will hold them, and the person to be in charge. Decide on whether to purchase in bulk (or get donated) the cloth and other basic materials, or whether to ask each participant to select and bring her/his own cloth and other needed items. There is often a price advantage in bulk purchases, and the quality control can be more assured. A disadvantage to bulk purchase is that all participants must work with the same page colors and the same basic formats.

Guide to fabric, sewing-machine, and craft stores for non-sewers

❧ Look in the Yellow Pages under "Fabric Shops" and "Craft Supplies."

❧ Call first to make sure they're still open and what hours.

❧ Look on the Notions "wall" of the store for crayons, fabric paints, packages of fusible web, buttons, etc.

❧ Ask where to find interfacing by the bolt. They are often stored under a cutting table. Not all brands are in every store.

❧ Look for a remnants or flat-fold table. These are left-over pieces of fabrics, ribbons, and laces sold at a cheaper price.

❧ Ask to be on the mailing list so you can be notified of upcoming sales.

❧ In chain stores look in the upholstery or home-decorating department for extra-wide fabric (60" [150cm] and wider), for heavier fabrics (canvas, tapestry, coarser weaves), and for special fabric (vinyl, plastic, laminated). Be sure to wash any fabrics you will be fusing, or the finishing treatment on the fabrics may prevent a good bond.

Note: Some fabrics shouldn't be pre-shrunk (which means to wash the fabric in warm water to let the fabric shrink before you cut it out). These fabrics usually have to be dry-cleaned. You might not want to use them in your book. Always check the end of the bolt for washing instructions.

Fig. 2-1. *The materials for making cloth books are inexpensive and readily available.*

Materials needed for a handmade cloth book

❖ Approximately 1 yd. (1m) of *quality* cloth, such as muslin or broadcloth, **at least 50% cotton,** 40" – 48" (102cm – 122 cm) wide for the pages. You will need less if fabric is 60" (150cm) wide. Before deciding on color and type of fabric, see "Selecting the Fabric" on page 17 and "Choosing a format" on page 25.

❖ Scraps of cloth in a wide variety of colors, prints, textures to decorate the pages. Ask friends who sew to give you scraps. Or buy old garments at rummage sales or thrift shops and cut them up. Fabric stores put ends of fabric in bins and call them remnants (see page 14). Also, watch for sheets on sale for pretty motifs.

❖ Fabric crayons, pens, or paints. I like *Pentel* and *Crayola* fabric crayons. Make sure the crayons, pens, or paint can be used on your cloth. Some take well only on 100% cotton; others take well on a mixture of cotton and polyester. Read the instructions to find out how yours perform.

❖ About 1 yd. (1m) of fusible web (two kinds, depending on intricacy—see page 34), available at fabric stores. Some brand names are: *Stitch Witchery, Wonder-Under,* and *HeatnBond.* (See chart on page 35.) You may also wish to try a tube of fabric adhesive (optional).

❖ Cotton cloths to use for pressing; old sheets are ideal.

❖ Approximately 1 yd. (1m) of heavy interfacing, available at fabric stores. Or, if you prefer, firm cardboard of the type used to back 8-1/2" by 11" (21.5cm by 28cm) pads of paper. See the section "Stiffening the pages" on page 64 before deciding whether you need stiffening and which type is recommended.

❖ 1 colored shoelace at least 28" (71cm) long

The following items are not absolutely necessary, but can add great variety to the design and attractiveness of cloth books:

Interesting buttons, beads, ribbons, lace and other decorations

Old or new zippers less than 8" (20.5cm) long; large snap fasteners

Bits of old fur or fake fur; small pieces of leather or vinyl

Flat molded plastic insects, animals, etc. These are usually available right before and after Halloween, in variety and toy stores

Velcro or other hook-and-loop type fasteners in dots or strips

Adhesive-backed mylar in gold, silver, etc. to make "mirrors"

Colored iron-on patches

Batting (if you wish to make a quilted book)

Equipment needed to make cloth books

Sharp scissors; embroidery scissors are ideal for detailed cutting

Pinking shears, if your fabric ravels

Iron and ironing board

Paper punch that makes sharp hole

Plastic see-through rulers

Crayon sharpener

Scratch paper and pencils

Tracing paper

Paper towels

Small plastic dishes for mixing crayon shavings, paints, etc.

Toothpick, for making dots with paint

A wide array of picture books to use as models. Borrow these from your local public library.

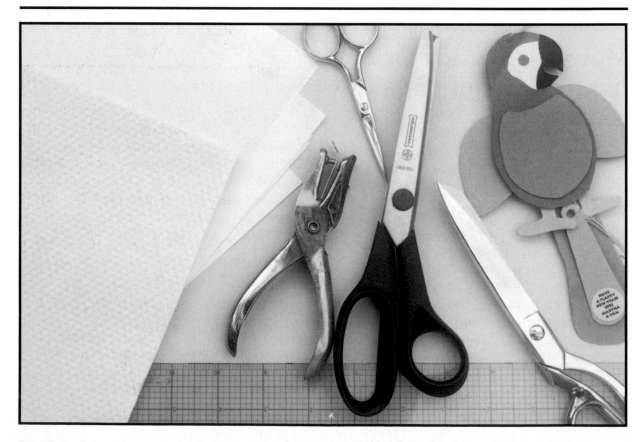

Fig. 2-2. *Assemble your supplies: paper, towels, scrap paper, paper punch, small sharp scissors, pinking shears, shears, ruler, and inspiration for patterns (coloring books, ads, favorite objects, etc.). (Scissors provided by Mundial.)*

Optional equipment, depending on techniques used

Teflon pressing sheet (very useful)—see page 37

Parchment paper from grocery store—see page 38

Needles, pins, and thread, if items are to be sewn on pages

Access to a sewing machine, if parts of book are to be machine-sewn

Overhead projector and acetate, or a slide projector, for transferring photo details to paper or cloth—see page 58

Clamps

Starch

Selecting the fabric

If purchasing in bulk, select a heavy muslin or broadcloth or similar smooth fabric in neutral light beige, white, or off-white, either 100% cotton or a blend of cotton (**at least 50%**) and polyester. If you prefer canvas, duck cloth, or denim, and find it at a price you can afford, you will probably not need any stiffening between the pages. However, if you wish to use folded-over pages that allow you to sew on appliqués, plastic creatures, etc., do not get fabric that is too heavy. Fold over an 8" (20.5cm) piece and see if the fold seems bulky. If it appears as though it would be hard to iron down the fold permanently, you might have difficulty working with the fabric.

If each participant is purchasing fabric individually, recommend the above types, or suggest they purchase the best quality they can find in a remnant or pre-cut piece at a fabric, craft, or variety store. The range of colors can be from pastels to fairly intense tones of blue, yellow, pink, or green. I once found a remnant of excellent quality, in a rich grass green. The piece, just under 2 yds. (1.85m), cost $3.98 and from it I made three books, all of which had gardens or lawns as their settings. The green color provided an ideal page color. (See *Let's Go Fishing*, page 1). The cloth was of a dense weave, 50% cotton, and needed no stiffening between the pages.

Important! Wash the cloth and let it hang dry, so as to remove the sizing. Otherwise, the other fabrics may not fuse well. This will also take care of any shrinkage problem.

Assembling the other materials

Have the person in charge and all prospective participants search for donated or inexpensive cloth scraps, discarded clothing items, old trimmings and the like.

Look for:

Cloth scraps in plain colors of all shades and intensities; prints with flowers, plants, or animal figures; prints with stripes or geometric shapes; braid, lace, and other trims.

Avoid:

More than 50% polyester, acetate, heavy wool, and any fabric that cannot be washed in cool water or ironed with a medium setting. Do not use colored felt if it is the type that bleeds when you wash it.

The person in charge of the group can buy the fusible web, crayons, pens, and paint, or inform the participants where they can purchase these items at the best prices in their area.

For a group of 15 persons, the following amounts are sufficient:

1 box (15 color size) of *Pentel Fabric Fun Dye Sticks*

1 box *Crayola Fabric Crayons*

1 set of fabric marking pens or two black laundry marking pens

12 yds. (11m) of fusible web; it is a good idea to have the paper-backed type (*Pellon Wonder-Under* is a well-known brand) and the type without backing (*Stitch Witchery* is perhaps the best-known brand).

Fig. 2-3. *Because the white clouds were already printed on this blue fabric, it was very easy to make a flap book, using the techniques described in Chapter 4.*

If you think there will be persons with an artistic bent in the group, who would like to mix their own colors for more subtlety, buy the following:

1 oz. (29.6ml) jars of *Deka* or other fabric paint in red, blue, yellow, white, black

If you are beginning a book project on your own, start with one box of fabric crayons and 1/2 yd (.5m) of each type of fusible web.

Do not buy the interfacing until you have determined whether you or any other participants need it. You may prefer other methods of stiffening the pages.

Collecting the equipment

For a group, the person in charge should determine what to ask each participant to bring so as to have sufficient quantities of sharp scissors, paper towels, pressing cloths, etc. Or the person in charge can assemble the equipment from sources available at the site where the group is to meet.

At least two irons and two ironing surfaces are needed for a group of 15. If some sewing techniques are to be used, one machine is usually sufficient. If the group consists of children, make sure an adult does all the ironing and sewing, or supervises closely at all times.

Selecting a site

Make sure you have enough table space to allow each participant to spread out and work freely. Generally, no more than two or three persons should work at each table.

Sites in or near public or school libraries are ideal, because this makes it easy to consult reference books and to look at a wide variety of children's books for inspiration.

3

Planning

This version (one of three) combines fabric collage and fabric paint. Based on photos of my brother-in-law's garden.

Making a paper dummy

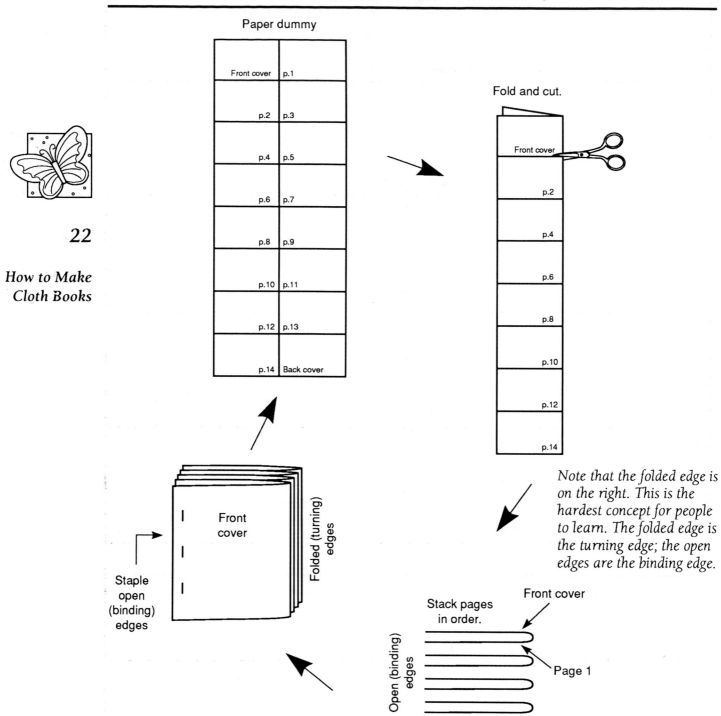

Paper dummy

Front cover	p.1
p.2	p.3
p.4	p.5
p.6	p.7
p.8	p.9
p.10	p.11
p.12	p.13
p.14	Back cover

Fold and cut.

Front cover
p.2
p.4
p.6
p.8
p.10
p.12
p.14

Note that the folded edge is on the right. This is the hardest concept for people to learn. The folded edge is the turning edge; the open edges are the binding edge.

Staple open (binding) edges
Front cover
Folded (turning) edges

Stack pages in order.
Front cover
Page 1
Open (binding) edges
Back cover

Time-saving tip for groups

The person in charge can photocopy enough sheets for the entire group, cut them on a paper-cutter, and have the miniature page dummies ready for the participants to use immediately. Tell the participants they are not required or restricted to using this number of pages.

To make a paper dummy, photocopy page 23. →

Fig. 3-3. How to make a paper dummy.

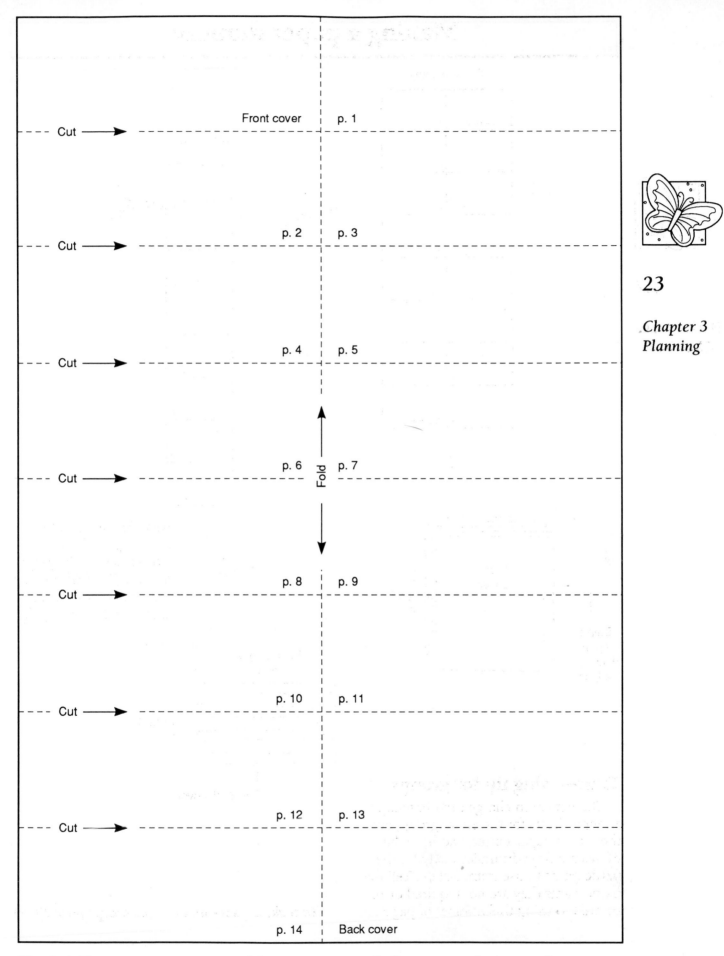

Fig. 3-4. *Photocopy as many copies of this page as you need. Then cut it up for a paper dummy.*

Be aware of flaps!

Make sure flaps don't interfere with objects on the facing page. Here is one such mistake I made in an early book I designed (see below).

The refrigerator and cupboard doors were both of vinyl and constantly stuck together when the book was closed. I should have placed the doors as far to the right on each page as possible. Then, when the book was closed, these items on facing pages would not be touching each other.

Notice that I was careful to hinge the refrigerator door on the left, so that when the page is opened up, the door is still closed. This allows the child to open it, and take out the milk (cloth in shape of milk carton, attached with hook-and-loop fastener). If the door were hinged on the right, it would open by itself in the process of turning the page, denying the child the fun of opening it.

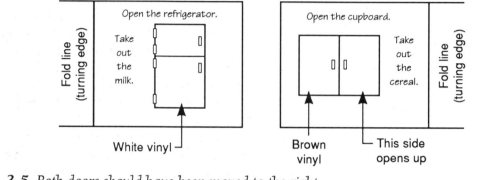

Fig. 3-5. Both doors should have been moved to the right.

Fig. 3-6. Marissa's well-loved book has flaps that open to show scenes. This is the back cover.

Choosing a format

Once you have a dummy, you are ready to choose a format, cut the fabric, and prepare patterns for illustrations. In most cases, it is easiest to make books that are 16 pages long (each side is a page). The measurements should be approximately

Horizontal format:
10" to 12" (25.5cm to 30.5cm) wide and 8" to 9" (20.5cm to 23cm) high

Vertical format:
8" to 9" (20.5cm to 23cm) wide and 10" to 12" (25.5cm to 30.5cm) high.

This makes a book easily managed by a child, not too thick, and with enough space to have large, clear illustrations.

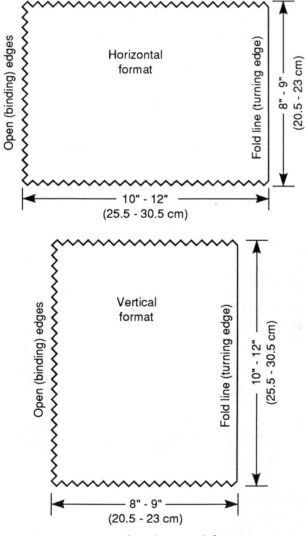

Fig. 3-7. *Horizontal and vertical format measurements.*

Of course, if the story line or the build-up of surprise needs more or fewer pages, by all means, adjust accordingly.

A folded page (one piece of cloth makes two sides) is generally a better idea than a single-thickness page, which can also have two sides but must be of much heavier fabric.

The fold should be on the *right-hand side* for books in English and other languages that you read from left to right. Should you be designing books in languages that you read from right to left, put the fold on the left-hand side of the page. If you wish to have a book that opens upward, rather than sideways, the folded edge should be at the bottom. (See the photo of *In Mrs. K's Classroom* on page 48). **In any case, the fold should be on the edge where you turn the page.**

Folded pages give extra body to the page. Furthermore, if the fabric is still limp even with the two thicknesses, you can slide cardboard as a stiffener into the fold, or use interfacing.

Still another reason for preferring folded pages is that you can sew items onto each side of the page, and the underside of the stitches will be hidden on the inside of the folded page.

Fig. 3-8. *Abby loves rainbows, so I created this puzzle book for her. Each page features articles of a different color, and the last page brings together all of the colors.*

Cutting the fabric pages

For some subjects, a small page is more appropriate. Also, some children prefer handling books not much bigger than their hands. If you wish to make a book of smaller size, you can get two small books from one yard (.095 meter) of cloth.

Cut the fabric in the following ways to get the format you want. Be sure the fabric has been washed and is ironed smooth. Leave the fold as it was down the middle when you purchased the fabric.

For a horizontal book:

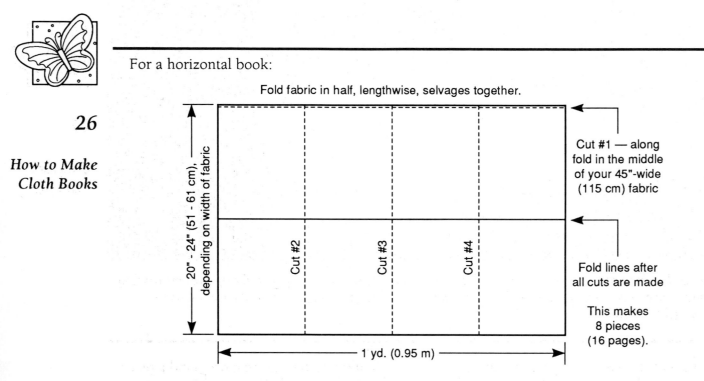

Fold fabric in half, lengthwise, selvages together.

20" - 24" (51 - 61 cm), depending on width of fabric

Cut #2   Cut #3   Cut #4

Cut #1 — along fold in the middle of your 45"-wide (115 cm) fabric

Fold lines after all cuts are made

This makes 8 pieces (16 pages).

1 yd. (0.95 m)

Fig. 3-9. *Make cuts in the order shown for a horizontal book.*

For a vertical book:

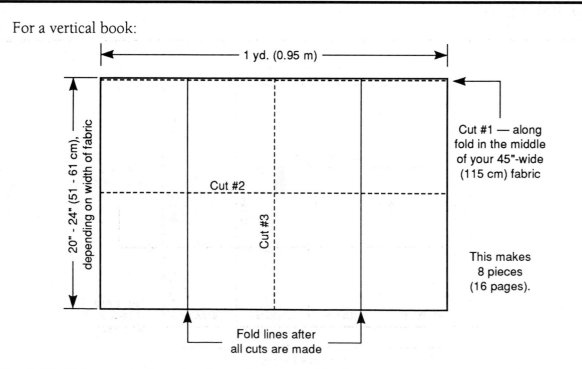

1 yd. (0.95 m)

20" - 24" (51 - 61 cm), depending on width of fabric

Cut #2

Cut #3

Cut #1 — along fold in the middle of your 45"-wide (115 cm) fabric

This makes 8 pieces (16 pages).

Fold lines after all cuts are made

Fig. 3-10. *Make cuts in the order shown for a vertical book.*

One day, out of the
cocoon came a
butterfly.
It fluttered off to
visit all the flowers
in grandpa's garden.

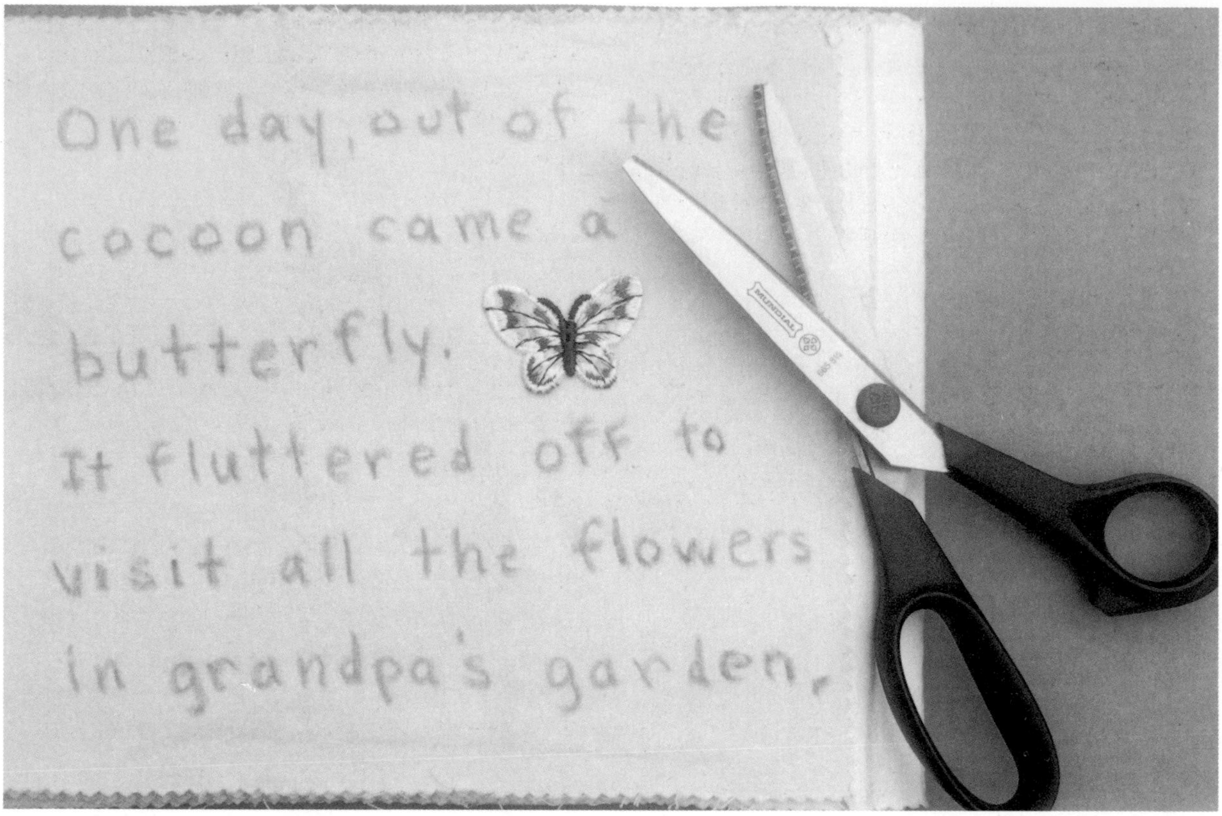

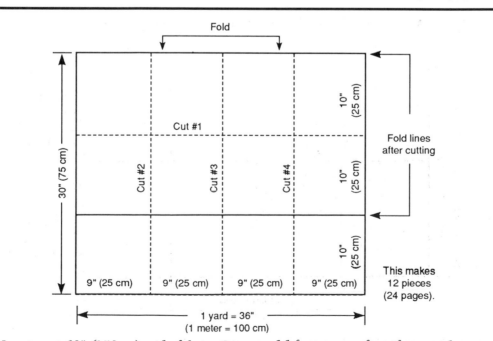

Fig. 3-11. *Pinking shears have tiny teeth that cut triangles in the raw edge and help prevent raveling. A much-used book like this one will always show a few threads along the pinked edge. (Scissors provided by Mundial.)*

It is best to use pinking shears for this cutting, so there is minimal raveling of the fabric. However, if you do not have pinking shears, you can finish the edges in other ways. (See page 66).

Should you by chance have found a piece of fabric that is 60" (150cm) wide, cut it in the following manner (Fig. 3-12). This will give you 12 double sides.

Fold
Cut #1
Cut #2
Cut #3
Cut #4
10" (25 cm)
10" (25 cm)
10" (25 cm)
Fold lines after cutting
30" (75 cm)
9" (25 cm)
9" (25 cm)
9" (25 cm)
9" (25 cm)
This makes 12 pieces (24 pages).
1 yard = 36"
(1 meter = 100 cm)

Fig. 3-12. *How to cut 60" (150cm) wide fabric. Cut a model from paper first if you wish.*

If your ideas can be expressed on slightly smaller pages, make Cuts 2, 3, and 4 only a fraction more than 9" (25cm) apart; make an additional Cut 5, also just a fraction wider than 9" (25cm). This will result in 15 double sides. You can then make two books, one of 16 pages (eight double sides) and one of 14 pages (seven double sides).

Once you have cut out all the cloth pages, fold them carefully (if they have folds) and iron them smooth. Line up the pages, one on top of the other. Check to see that the edges are fairly even, and trim as necessary.

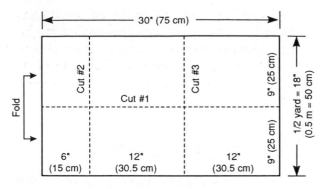

Fig. 3-14. For heavy fabric, you do not need to make a fold. Cut as shown.

This will give you 10 pieces, each 9" by 12" (25cm by 30.5cm). You may use them in either a horizontal or vertical format. Press them and make sure all sides line up evenly.

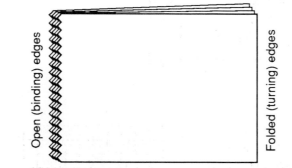

Fig. 3-13. *Stack folded pages and trim as necessary. The folded edge is to the right in this example. The folded edge is the* **turning** *edge.*

This will be the approximate size of your finished book. Thickness will increase somewhat, depending on how you illustrate the pages.

Also, if you intend to quilt the pages, the thickness will double. Make sure that you do not make the book too thick and bulky for a child to handle comfortably. If you have not yet made a paper dummy of your book and wish to do so, put the cloth pages aside and make a plan for your book. See page 20.

Working with heavy fabric

If you have a heavy piece of fabric that does not fold well, and you do not wish to do any sewing at all, you must cut out each page in exactly the finished size you want. The pages will not be folded over to make two pages. Such heavy fabrics generally come in widths of 60" (152cm). You will need only a half-yard (50cm) of fabric. Using pinking shears, cut it this way:

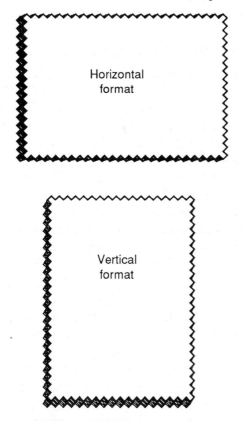

Fig. 3-15. *Horizontal and vertical formats.*

If you do not have access to pinking shears, cut with regular scissors, but in that case you must be sure to reinforce the right hand edge of each page (the turning edge). If you do not, the cloth will likely ravel from the child's frequent turning of the pages. You might have to finish the other edges as well, depending on how tightly the fabric is woven. See the section "Finishing the page edges" on page 66.

Remember, you will not be able to do any sewing or writing on these pages that might show through to the other side. Each side will be a finished page. There will be no hidden back sides, as there are in the folded pages shown earlier.

Making your own patterns for illustrations

In Chapter 4, you'll learn how to prepare fabrics used as illustrations. Cutting out a flower or teddy bear already printed on fabric and putting it directly in your book is the easiest way to create an illustration. But you can't always find what you want printed on fabric. These instructions are for ways to create a pattern for any illustration you need.

Drawing and tracing

Many times you will find a scrap of cloth the right color for the figure you wish to represent in an illustration, but you feel you cannot draw well enough to make it recognizable. Using scrap paper, draw an outline of the figure in the size you wish to have it, cut it out, and place it on the page. If it looks all right in proportion to the size of the page, but you are still not satisfied with the shape of the figure, search for a similar figure in a book or coloring book, and trace the outline on tracing paper. Cut out the pattern in paper and again see how it looks on the page. If you are going to make your figure in cloth, transfer the pattern to the paper side of paper-backed fusible web, remembering to reverse the pattern. If you are going to make your figure in paint or crayon, trace the pattern outline onto the fabric using dressmaker's pencil or pens of the fade-away type.

Or you can trace the pattern on acetate and transfer it to cloth by means of an overhead projector, as described on page 59. Patterns found in sewing or craft stores, coloring books, or handbooks on illustrating and bookmaking might help you design just the pages you want. Libraries also have lots of children's books and magazines with patterns.

However, try to use mostly your own imagination and efforts, rather than resorting to too much tracing. The more patterns you make, the better you will get. Always save your patterns, in case you need to use them again.

If you see a small pattern and need to enlarge it, use graph paper or any paper ruled in squares.

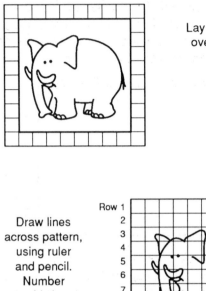

Lay pattern over grid.

29

Chapter 3
Planning

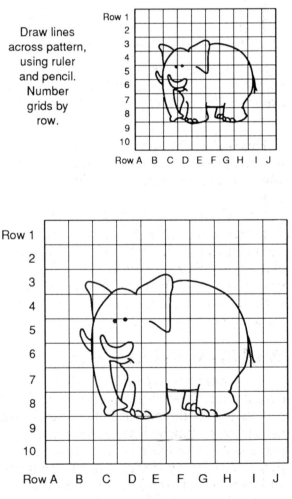

Draw lines across pattern, using ruler and pencil. Number grids by row.

Decide how much bigger you want the design and make a grid that large. Copy the pattern lines one grid at a time, beginning at the upper left.

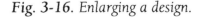

Fig. 3-16. Enlarging a design.

Oh! No! Coming toward him were ten children, chasing him away.

Fig. 3-17. *Two pages from* Tortoise Takes a Trip, *inspired by a workshop in Mauritius and by an earlier printed book produced at a workshop in Fiji.*

Or use the overhead projector method explained on page 59. Some copy machines can enlarge designs, too.

Sometimes you need to repeat a figure, but want it to look different. In making a book for a workshop in Mauritius, I needed to show 10 children running after a turtle. I am poor at making individual facial expressions, so I cut out the same running-child figure 10 times, and gave each individuality by putting on different bits of clothing. Actually, the effect is much like watching a group of children on a beach in Mauritius, with the sun over them so bright it blots out all the facial details. The children loved the book and didn't notice my inferior drawing skills.

Transferring photos

Full instructions for transferring photos directly to cloth start on page 58. If you want to make a pattern of a person, scene, house, or room, you can project a slide or a drawing by slide projector or opaque projector onto paper pinned to the wall.

Books in different formats

Once you have created a book or two, experiment with different formats. You may even prefer to cut your fabric into interesting shapes that suit the proposed content of your book, such as stars or circles.

One of the easiest-to-make books I constructed started out with a piece of canvas 37" by 12" (94cm by 30cm). I cut and folded it in the following way:

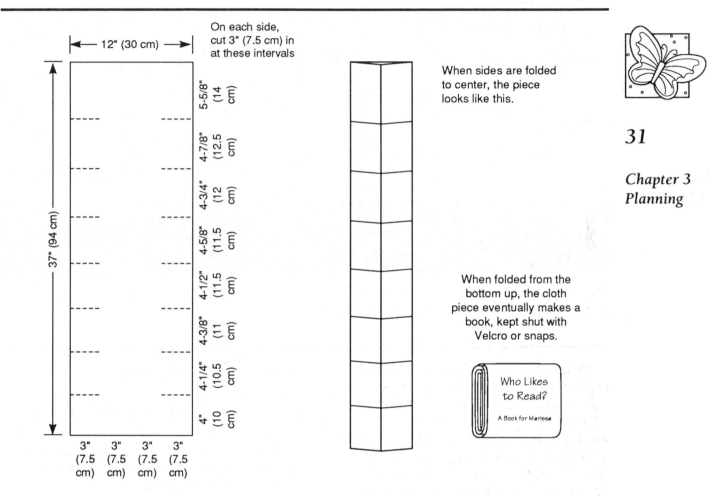

On each side, cut 3" (7.5 cm) in at these intervals

5-5/8" (14 cm)
4-7/8" (12.5 cm)
4-3/4" (12 cm)
4-5/8" (11.5 cm)
4-1/2" (11.5 cm)
4-3/8" (11 cm)
4-1/4" (10.5 cm)
4" (10 cm)

12" (30 cm)

37" (94 cm)

3" (7.5 cm)   3" (7.5 cm)   3" (7.5 cm)   3" (7.5 cm)

When sides are folded to center, the piece looks like this.

When folded from the bottom up, the cloth piece eventually makes a book, kept shut with Velcro or snaps.

Who Likes to Read?
A Book for Marissa

Fig. 3-18. Another format for a cloth book.

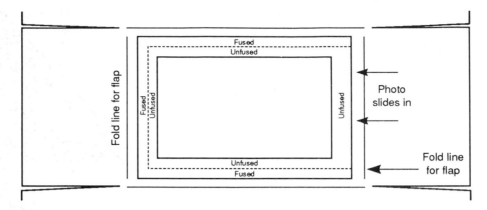

Fig. 3-19. *How to make slots for photographs.*

Under each of the flaps, I made a *cloth mat*, 3" by 5" (7.5cm by 12.5cm), to frame a photo. I fused only the outer edge of the mat to the canvas. I left unfused the inner edge of the mat, plus the entire right edge, so that a photo could be slid into the resulting cloth frame. See page 52 for more information on making slots for photographs.

Fig. 3-20. *This hastily constructed book was made just for the fun of it for my grandniece Marissa, age 2.*

Fig. 3-21 *The unfolding and opening of the flaps fascinated Marissa; the silly text, full of puns, was meant to be enjoyed by adults reading it to her.*

Making

A lift-the-flap book using a fabric printed with clouds. The front and back cover text was written in cursive, to suggest skywriting.

Making

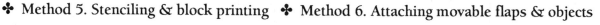

34

*How to Make
Cloth Books*

Although both text and illustrations are important in a children's book, it is often the illustrations that seem most difficult for an ordinary person to plan and create. Do not hesitate to make a book just because you consider yourself a person with few artistic talents. If you can dress yourself in attractive, color-coordinated clothes, you have enough creative talent to make a cloth book for a child. Just select one of the seven techniques in this chapter to create a variety of pictures.

Method 1.
Iron-on appliqué using fusible web

Fusing non-intricate shapes

Some marvelous new craft products make the job of illustrating a cloth book easy. The fusible webs are thin sheets of glue that allow you to attach cloth to cloth with no sewing. Now you can illustrate a book with motifs cut from fabric—boats, animals, fish, flowers, etc.

There are two types of fusible web:

1. The plain fusible web, with brand names such as *Stitch Witchery* and *Wonder Web*, is a gossamer-like web that is usually found in fabric and craft stores in bolts that are 12" (30.5cm), 18" (46cm), or 24" (61cm) wide. It also comes in narrow rolls suitable for hemming or edging.

2. The paper-backed fusible web, available under such brand names as *HeatnBond, Magic Fuse, Stitch Witchery Plus, TransBond, TransWeb,* and *Wonder-Under,* comes with a paper backing, also in 12" (30.5cm), 18" (46cm), or 24" (61cm) widths.

I have paid from $.98 to $2.69 per yard for these fusible webs, depending on the store and special sales.

Use the plain fusible web only with shapes that are fairly easy to cut around. Do not use it with fabric pieces that you intend to cut into very intricate shapes. If you have a piece with intricate edges, or quite a number of small pieces, it is better to use the paper-backed fusible web.

How to use plain fusible web

Let us say you have a flower cut out of an old dress that you wish to bond to a page of your book. The flower is an oval shape with no intricate edges. Place the cloth flower, right side up, over the fusible web. Pin within the flower. Using sharp scissors, cut out the

Fusible Web Chart

Manu-facturer	Product Name	Paper-backed?	Fusing Temperature			Dry or Steam?	Washable?	Sewable?	Comments
			Silk	Wool	Cotton				
Aleene's	Aleene's Hot Stitch Fusible Web	Yes		X		Dry	Yes	Yes	
Dritz	Magic Fuse	Yes		X		Steam	Yes	Yes	
HTC Handler	Stitch Witchery	No		X		Steam	Yes	Yes	
	TransWeb	Yes		X		Steam	Yes	Yes	
	Stitch Witchery Plus	Yes		X		Steam	Yes	Yes	New
	TransBond	Yes		X		Steam	Yes	Yes	For crafts
Pellon	Wonder-Under	Yes		X		Steam	Yes	Yes	All can be used with anything porous (cardboard, etc.)
	Heavy-Duty Wonder-Under	Yes		X		Steam	Yes	Yes	
	Wonder-Web	No		X		Steam	Yes	Yes	
Sew Art	AppliHesive	Yes		X	X	Dry	Yes	Yes	Heavy weight—holds more firmly
Solar-Kist	Fine Fuse	No	X	X	X	Dry	Yes	Yes	
	Tuf-Fuse	No	X	X	X	Dry	Yes	Yes	
Therm O Web	HeatnBond Original	Yes	X			Dry	Yes	No	No-sew version
	HeatnBond Lite	Yes	X			Dry	Yes	Yes	Sewing version

Fig. 4-1.

flower. The fusible web should now be the exact same size and shape as your flower.

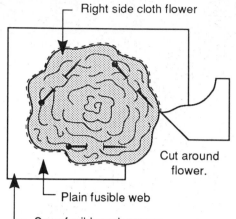

Fig. 4-2. *Cut the plain fusible web the same size as the motif.*

Do not discard the bits and pieces of fusible web that you cut away in making the shape that exactly matches your cloth figure. Have an old plastic dish, plastic bag, or an envelope handy and slip these bits of fusible web into it. These bits will be useful when you need small pieces to bond tiny corners. You can also scatter the bits to bond larger pieces.

Place the flower, with the fusible web under it, in the position on the page where you wish to bond it permanently. Remove the pin. If this is the only item to be bonded to the page, iron as described on page 39.

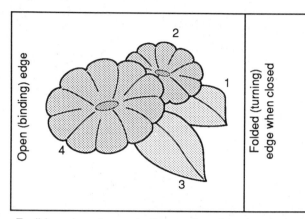

Fusible web under each piece—place in order shown.

Fig. 4-3. *Overlapping shapes are fused from the bottom up.*

Fig. 4-4. *Fusible webs make it easy to construct cloth books. From left: plain fusible web, paper-backed fusible web, Dritz Hem-n-Tape, and pre-cut paper-backed fusible web. You can see the web separated from the paper at the end. Under all is a Teflon sheet.*

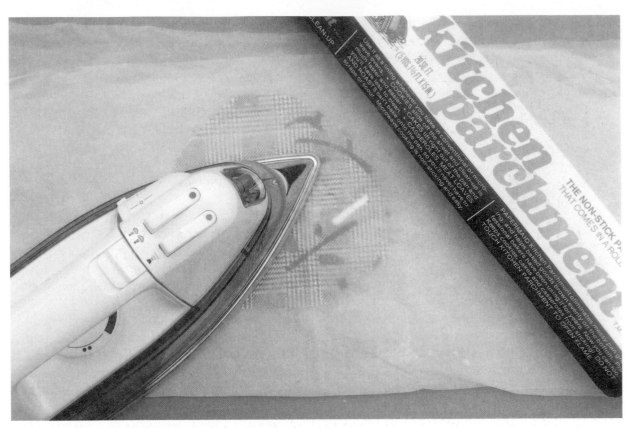

Fig. 4-5. *Plain fusible web is placed on half of the Teflon sheet. Fabric is placed over the web. Then the other half of the Teflon sheet is folded over. The heat of the iron fuses the web to the fabric, but the web does not stick to the Teflon sheet. Now the fabric can be fused to a background.*

However, to create the complete illustration, it is likely you have several pieces you wish to bond on that page. You can iron-bond them all at the same time. Cut a fusible web pattern for each non-intricate piece you wish to bond. Make sure the right side of the fabric to be bonded is facing up in all cases. Place the fabric pieces and fusible web in the positions you wish to have them on the page. When you have placed the entire illustration, iron as described in the section "Fusing the appliqué pieces to the background," page 38.

A new product called a *Teflon* pressing sheet has made the use of plain fusible web much easier. It looks like a piece of milky plastic and comes in various sizes (see Mail-order supply list on page 87). Plain fusible web does not stick to the pressing sheet. This means you can use plain fusible web as you do paper-backed fusible web. You put the plain fusible web directly on half of the *Teflon* pressing sheet, place the fabric over it, cover with the other half, and press. Make sure the fusible web is not larger than the fabric or it will stick to your iron. (Or you can sandwich the fusible web and fabric between the

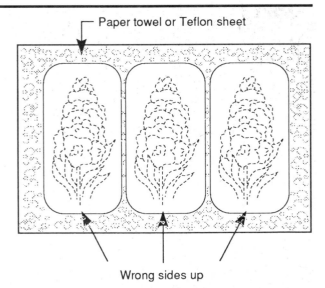

Paper towel or Teflon sheet

Wrong sides up

Fig. 4-6. *To use paper-backed fusible web, start by laying fabric wrong side up on paper towel or Teflon sheet.*

folded-over *Teflon* pressing sheet.) When the fabric cools, you can pull it off the pressing sheet. The fusible web now covers the back of your fabric so that you can iron your fabric piece onto another fabric.

Flash! As we went to press, Nancy Ward, author of *Fabric Painting Made Easy* (Chilton Book Company, 1993), showed us how ordinary parchment paper, bought in a roll at the grocery store, acts like a *Teflon* pressing sheet. I still love my *Teflon* sheet.

If you accidentally fuse plain fusible web to your iron or ironing board, either remove it with rubbing alcohol (let the iron cool, of course) or by ironing onto a sheet of un-scented fabric softener.

How to use paper-backed fusible web

It's easiest to bond a large area of fabric with paper-backed fusible web, then cut out what you want. But this may waste areas of fabric and fusible web.

Let us assume that you are going to cut out a piece of fabric with smaller flowers, each with an intricate pattern of leaves and petals. Cut an oval or rectangular shape around the entire pattern on the fabric. If you have a number of such pieces, cut them all in similar ovals or rectangles.

Lay the fabric pieces, **wrong side up**, side by side on a paper towel or on a Teflon pressing sheet spread out on your ironing surface. Leave as little space as you possibly can between the fabric pieces.

Now, cut a piece of paper-backed fusible web just large enough to cover all of these fabric pieces. Place this fusible web, paper side up, directly over the fabric pieces.

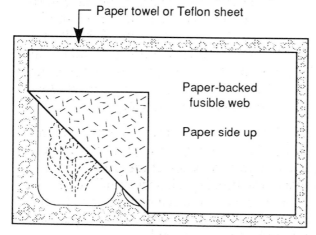

Fig. 4-7. *Cover the fabric with paper-backed fusible web, glue side against wrong side of fabric, and press.*

Ironing the fusible web to the appliqué fabric

Place a heated iron directly on the paper side of the web. For the heat setting, follow the instructions given with the fusible web (see chart on page 35). Generally, the wool setting without steam is recommended. Keep the iron in place for the recommended amount of time, usually a few seconds. Avoid moving the iron from side to side. Lift up the iron.

To check the bond, pick up the paper backing. The fabric pieces should be attached to it. If the paper towel also got attached because edges of the fusible web touched it, gently remove it. If you used the *Teflon* sheet, it will lift away.

Let the fabric, now attached to the paper-backed fusible web, cool completely. **If you intend to trace and cut out your own patterns, do not remove the paper backing yet.** When it is cool, take hold of an edge of each of the fabric pieces and pull away. You will then have separate cloth pieces, each with fusible web bonded to the back (or a large piece of fabric entirely covered on the back with fusible web, if you fused the entire width).

If the fabric has the patterns you want already pre-printed in it, cut around the figures in just the way you wish to have them appear on your page. For the book *In the Rain*

Fig. 4-8. *This page from* In the Rain Forest *appears to be cut out from one fabric piece but is actually many bits cut and placed to create the scene. A black cat hides behind a liftable flap.*

Forest, for example, I cut around various scenes printed on a commercially available fabric. I then placed them, collage style, in such a way that each page appears to be a miniature scene from a rain forest.

Do not restrict yourself to simply cutting out already existing designs or figures printed on cloth. Experiment with making your own. If you wish, make patterns in paper first. (See the section "Making your own patterns for illustrations" on page 29).

If you are using your own pattern, sketch or trace the pattern outline on the paper backing of the fusible web (after it has been fused to the fabric). Then cut around design. Use very sharp, pointed scissors, so all corners can be reached easily.

After you have cut out the figures and separated the paper backing from the fabric, lay the figures on the page in precisely the positions you wish to have them in your final illustration.

Fusing appliqué pieces to the background

Adjust the pieces so they are in the exact places you want them to be on the page. Double-check against your dummy (see page 20) to be sure you are placing them on the proper side of the page. You can place an illustration close to the folded edge of a page, but allow at least 2" of margin on the open edge (the binding edge—usually the left edge). If you have used both types of fusible web, make sure the loose pieces of fusible web are exactly lined up under their appropriate fabric pieces.

You now have all of the pieces of your illustration in place. If you have used only fabrics that can withstand the heat of a wool setting on your iron, you may now proceed to bond them in place. Heat your iron to the wool or cotton setting (as recommended by the instructions for your fusible web). If you have used heat-sensitive materials, consult the section on "Bonding vinyls and other special fabrics" on page 40.

Dampen a cotton press cloth large enough to cover the page. Lay it gently over your entire illustration. Place the hot iron over the press cloth in the center of the illustration and leave it in place for the number of seconds recommended by the manufacturer of your fusible web. Do not move the iron back and forth. If you cannot cover the entire illustration with the surface of the iron, first bond the central part of the illustration, then lift up the iron and put it down over the remaining parts.

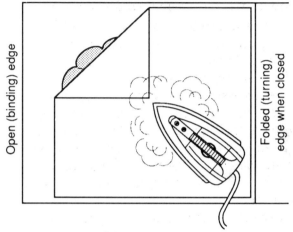

Fig. 4-9. *Cover fabric with press cloth. Don't slide iron; lift it up and down.*

Caution: This is sometimes tricky because the iron, when lifted up, also occasionally lifts up or moves the press cloth. This in turn sometimes moves the illustration pieces out of place. If you have intricate areas that are likely to move out of place easily, bond that area of the illustration first. Another method is to touch the center of all the pieces with the tip of the iron first. This lightly tacks them all down to keep them from moving.

Lift away the iron; then lift away the press cloth. Do not worry if the press cloth has stuck slightly to some of the pattern edges where the fusible web accidentally extended beyond the fabric piece being bonded. The press cloth will easily come away if you take it off while the fabric is still hot.

If you have a design in which various pieces of fabric overlap each other, do them in order, sewing the bottom layer first, and continuing until each layer is finished. For example, for a large pattern of leaves and flowers, you might sew in this manner:

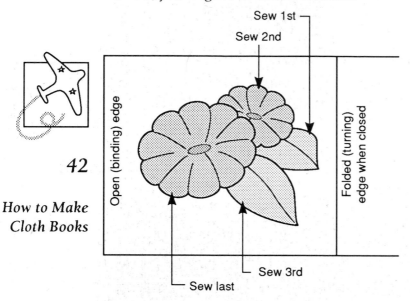

Fig. 4-12. As in fusing, overlapping shapes are applied from the bottom up.

Machine sewing

In machine appliqué, you can turn under the seam allowance and use a straight stitch to attach the fabric to the backing. You will get an effect similar to the running hand-stitch, above. A much more polished and attractive effect can be achieved by using satin stitching, or one of the zigzag patterns that are now possible on many sewing machines. Do not add a seam allowance if you satin-stitch. Have most of the stitches fall on the appliqué, not on the backing. For best results, use a size 80(14) needle and a fine thread, like machine-embroidery thread (see Mail-order supply list on page 87). Put typing-weight paper or tear-away stabilizer (ask at your fabric store or see Mail-order supply list) under the backing for support. After satin-stitching, tear away the stabilizer. In most cases you will sew on the outer, finished side of the page rather than on the underside. Because you don't need a seam allowance

with satin stitching, you can use a variety of heavier fabrics in machine appliqué, but be aware that they might be more difficult to handle.

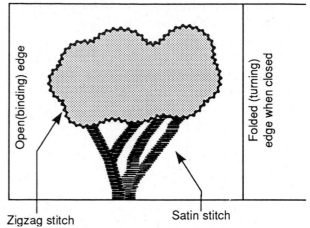

Fig. 4-13. Machine appliqué.

Be sure to pull through all thread ends and tie them on the inner side of the page.

The hand-made cloth books designed by Isis Valeria and made in Brazil, and the books produced by Marla Ostrowski, are beautiful examples of machine-sewn appliqué. (See photo on page 43.)

Method 3. Quilted appliqué

If you are skilled in quilting techniques, you can make each page a miniature appliquéd quilt. Treat the page like a quilt top. Prepare the appliqués as described in the previous section.

Or you might decide to transfer photos to cloth and quilt around them, using the techniques suggested in "Transferring photos to cloth" on page 58. Remember to leave enough fabric around the photo to turn under when you appliqué it.

Cut out your appliqué patterns or transferred photos; then press or tack under the edges. Place the pieces in position on the page. Again, make sure you save a sufficient margin on the open edges of the page for binding later.

Fig. 4-14. *Inside page from* Au Au Lambau, *one of a series designed and produced in Brazil. The collage illustrations are satin-stitched by machine. The dog has Velcro behind it and can stick to various positions in the book.*

Fig. 4-15. *Page from* Country Countdown (*Butterick Pattern 4837*) *sewn by Marla Ostrowski.*

Children love finding things in pockets. If you wish to place a pocket with a lift-up flap on one of your pages, cut out a piece of fabric slightly larger than the space you have for the pocket on the page; then cut out a rectangle for the flap, making sure you have enough fabric to turn under on all sides.

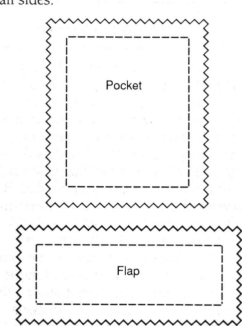

Pocket

Flap

Fig. 4-16. *Children love pockets and flaps in cloth books.*

Once the pieces are cut out, turn under the allowances and press or baste them, whichever you prefer. (Or if you prefer a different effect and the fabric doesn't ravel, don't turn under the edges.) Stitch any edges that need to be sewn before the pieces are sewn into place, such as the top edge of the pocket or all around the flap. Be sure to position the flap far enough above the pocket that an item can slide easily into the pocket.

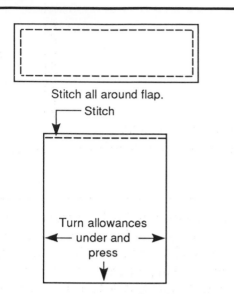

Stitch all around flap.
Stitch

Turn allowances
under and
press

Fig. 4-17. *Be sure to position flap far enough away from pocket so that an item can slide inside easily.*

Now place the pieces on the page in the position you wish to have the pocket and pin it into place. Using either a running stitch, a whip stitch, or a blanket stitch (or any other favorite stitch), attach the pieces to the page, sewing around three sides..

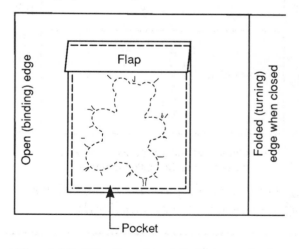

Open (binding) edge

Flap

Folded (turning) edge when closed

Pocket

Fig. 4-18. *Wonder what is hidden inside this pocket?*

For experienced sewers, many wonderful ideas for making pockets are in the book *Sew Any Patch Pocket* by Claire B. Shaeffer, published by Open Chain (see page 74).

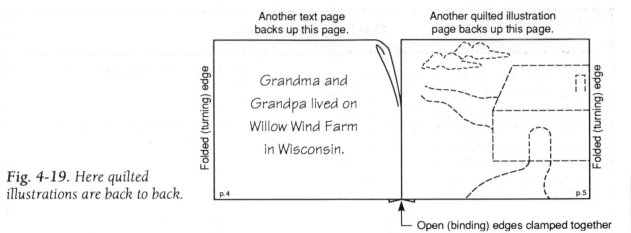

Another text page backs up this page.

Another quilted illustration page backs up this page.

Folded (turning) edge

Grandma and
Grandpa lived on
Willow Wind Farm
in Wisconsin.

Folded (turning) edge

p.4

p.5

Fig. 4-19. Here quilted illustrations are back to back.

Open (binding) edges clamped together

45

*Chapter 4
Making*

Because quilting makes a very bulky book, try designing your book so that illustrations are quilted back to back. Text can be on the unquilted facing pages. This way you have two pages of text back-to-back, then two pages of illustrations back-to-back, etc. You need batting only the size of a page (half of the folded fabric). Fold the fabric over the batting and quilt both sides at the same time.

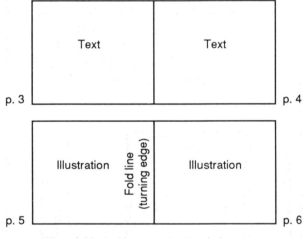

Text	Text

p. 3 | p. 4

| Illustration | Fold line (turning edge) | Illustration |

p. 5 | p. 6

When folded with cotton batting in between, the pages can be quilted together.

Fig. 4-20. When the pages are assembled, the back-to-back quilted pages look like this.

If this creates difficulties in quilting, and you prefer to have text always on the left and the illustration on the right, quilt only the side with the illustration. Use a thin cotton backing material under the batting, adding the batting and backing to the underside of the page and only under the illustration side. Do the quilting with the pages unfolded. Be sure to write the text for the next illustration while the page is still open flat (Fig. 4-19).

To begin quilting, tack all three layers (page, batting, backing) together at the four corners. Use a hoop or other type of frame designed for lap quilting. Place it around the middle part of your illustration and begin your quilting. If you prefer, and are skilled at it, use machine quilting. Always begin quilting from the middle part of your design, gradually working your way to the outer edges. Because these are small pages, you need to stitch only around outlines of the figures. This will be sufficient for the page to hold its shape. Other smaller details can be outlined, if desired. Plan the text to coordinate with the design of the quilting line (Fig. 4-21).

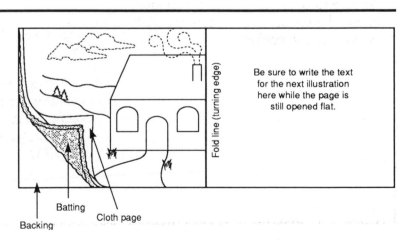

Be sure to write the text for the next illustration here while the page is still opened flat.

Fold line (turning edge)

Backing

Batting

Cloth page

Fig. 4-21. Another variation of quilted illustrations calls for quilting before folding the page.

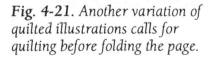

Trapunto quilting

If you have just one or two figures on each page that you wish to emphasize, you might want to try trapunto. In this case, cut a piece of batting just slightly smaller than the figure. Place it under the fabric figure before you appliqué it to the page. This gives a puffy, three-dimensional look to the figure.

Trapunto is especially effective with fabric squares that already have one large figure printed on them, set within a frame or square. For example, see *Marissa's Bedtime Book* (Fig. 4-22).

Method 4. Drawing or painting directly on fabric

Recently there has been an explosion of crayon and paint products designed for use on fabrics. If used properly, these can be very effective and long-lasting. I like to combine them with cloth appliqué, for contrast. However, if you are good at drawing, painting or even tracing, you may wish to make your entire book using this method.

Because I am not good at drawing faces with individuality, and yet want to include portraits of specific individuals, I often project photos or slides onto the actual cloth by means of an overhead projector or slide projector (see page 59). I then trace the image. This enables me to get a fairly accurate outline of the face of the particular person I wish to depict. For specific outdoor or indoor scenes I also sometimes use photos or slides as models, especially if I want certain details to be in a particular perspective. (See, for example, *In Mrs. K's Classroom* on page 47).

If you sketch in your design with pencil, be aware that even very light strokes will often show through the color of the paint. You might experiment with such pens as the *Fade-Away*, by White.

Once you have sketched in your design, decide what type of crayons or paint you wish to use. Fabric crayons are easier to handle in covering large areas. Fabric paint or pens are better for filling in tiny details. However, some fabric pens bleed into the surrounding

Fig. 4-22. *Trapunto quilting outlines the key figure on each page of this bedtime book, giving it a soft, puffy look and feel.*

Fig. 4-23. *Craft and fabric stores carry lots of supplies to help you make pictures for your cloth books: collections of patterns, fabric dye sticks, permanent markers, fabric crayons, and transfer pens.*

Fig. 4-24. *Slides were taken of many views in Mrs. K's actual pre-school classroom, then projected onto paper to make patterns. The dress-up clothes rack is shown in a perspective similar to what the children see in class.*

cloth, and some are permanent from the moment they are applied to cloth. If the manufacturer's instructions are not clear, test on scraps before using in your final illustration.

Please note: School crayons are the not the same as fabric crayons. Your box must say "Fabric Crayons" for this to work.

Tack or pin the cloth taut and crayon or paint in one direction only. Add shadings and details after you have filled in background colors. Be careful not to touch the surrounding cloth while handling the paint or crayons. If you accidentally brush against it, or spill paint, or crayon in an incorrect detail, you can wash out your error by using cool water and a mild detergent, provided you are using crayons or paints that need heat before being set permanently. Rinse thoroughly, pat out the excess water with a towel, and let the cloth page hang dry. Do not attempt to iron it dry. Instead, work on another page.

Several copies of the same design

If you wish to make several copies of the same design, use crayons or pens to trace or color the design. One brand is called *Sulky Iron-on Transfer Pen.* Ask your fabric store for it or see the Mail-order supply list on page 87.

On drawing paper make the design with transfer pen and crayon it in, using thick, firm strokes.

Caution: The drawing will transfer in the reverse, so don't use letters, unless you reverse them.

Place the drawing, design side down, in the position on the first page where you wish it to appear. Iron on the reverse side of the paper. Lift up the drawing, let the paper cool, redraw the design, and iron it on the second page where you wish it to appear. Continue for as many times as you wish to use the design. See "Heat-setting and removing errors" on page 49. In this case you are automatically setting the design and cannot wash it out.

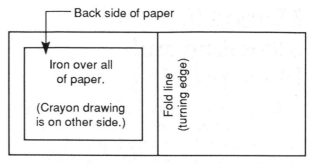

Fig. 4-25. *To make several copies of one design, draw it on paper and iron it onto cloth.*

Adding texture and detail to crayons and paint

Use a sharpener to give points to the crayons if you need them for detailed work. Save the shavings by separate colors in small plastic dishes. When you need texture for a roof, or flowers, or any other object, sprinkle on the appropriate color of shavings. Place a paper towel over the design and iron on as described on page 62. You can get interesting color and texture by experimenting.

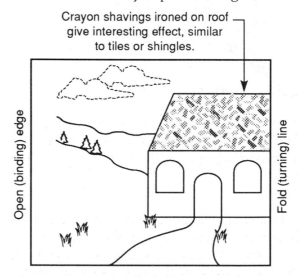

Fig. 4-26. *Crayon shavings can give interesting textures.*

Method 5.
Stenciling and block printing

If you have found some stencils you would like to use, or have experience in making your own stencils, then fabric paint is your best medium. Tack the cloth page down tautly, then tack or tape down the stencil in the correct position on the page. Use a soft stenciling brush, and be sparing of paint. Dab it on with a circular, twisting motion.

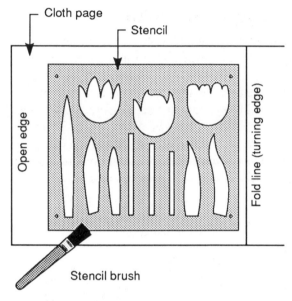

Fig. 4-27. *Choose the shape you wish to stencil, place it on the page, and dab paint on. Move the stencil carefully to align the next shape you wish to use.*

Rubber stamps or other stamps or blocks already available to you can also be reproduced on cloth using fabric paint. Or you can create your own block prints using potatoes, styrofoam, cork, leaves, flower heads or other material.

If you are stenciling or block printing throughout a book, plan the entire book and then stencil or print each color in turn, wherever possible. This will save you from having to mix colors more than once. It will also mean less washing of brushes.

Use only a moderate amount of paint on the stamping surface. After brushing paint on the item, tilt to the side to see if the paint runs or drips. If it does, there is too much paint.

Heat-setting and removing errors

Virtually all fabric crayons, paints, or pens must be set with heat. To remove an error, you have to wash it out *before* it is ironed. If you make a mistake and don't want to wash out the entire drawing, carefully place paper under and over the parts of the drawing that *are correct* and iron them at the recommended setting. Then wash out your error in the part you did not iron.

Remember, when your drawing or painting is complete, in most cases it needs to be set with heat. Place paper towels **under and over** the page, and iron at the heat-setting recommended for the crayons or paints you are using. **Use dry heat**, unless directed otherwise in the instructions. For areas of heavy crayoning, you may need to change the paper towels three or four times. Keep on testing until no more crayon comes off on the paper towels during the heat-setting process.

Method 6.
Attaching movable flaps and objects

Flaps

Children love the surprise of opening up tiny doors, windows or flaps in a book; they also like to manipulate an object in some way. You can often plan your illustrations in such a way that they have these movable parts.

I like to make doors out of fabric that suggests a texture of wood, enamel or metal. Doubling the fabric gives it extra strength for the many times it will be handled by children opening the flap. The doors can be attached by sewing in the spots where the hinges would be, or by using a strip of fusible web (if the fabric is not too heat-sensitive).

Always make sure the opening side of the door (where the handle would be if you

Fig. 4-28a and b. In Mrs. K's Classroom *opens upward. Behind the door, the children discover a photo of Mrs. K herself. Inside are many more flaps, with photos underneath. The photos can be changed each year for each new class of students.*

Fig. 4-29. *Pages from* My Clown Book. *The child can manipulate something on each page. The washing machine door opens toward the turning edge.*

attached one) is **farthest from the outside folded edge** of the page. This will allow the turning of the page without having the door flip open.

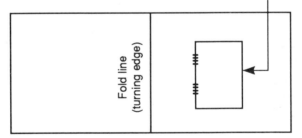

Fig. 4-30. *Point door flap openings away from the turning edge.*

I sometimes like to attach doors with hinges made from tiny bits of plastic tubing that I recycled from a shopping bag handle. I sew through the tubes. But sewing with black thread directly into the fabric at the hinge points is also satisfactory. If I find a tiny round button of just the right size, I attach it as a handle.

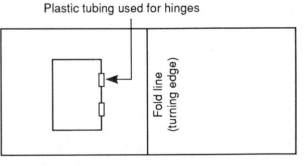

Fig. 4-31. *Door hinges can be made of small plastic tubes.*

To make a flap, cut fusible web of the exact shape of your flap pattern, or use a piece of fabric that has had paper-backed fusible web already fused to it.

Cut a piece of backing cloth for the upper, lower, or side two-thirds of the pattern, depending on whether you wish to have the flap open up, down, or sideways. This will leave a small portion of the fusible web free to bond to the page. The remainder of the piece will be bonded to the flap.

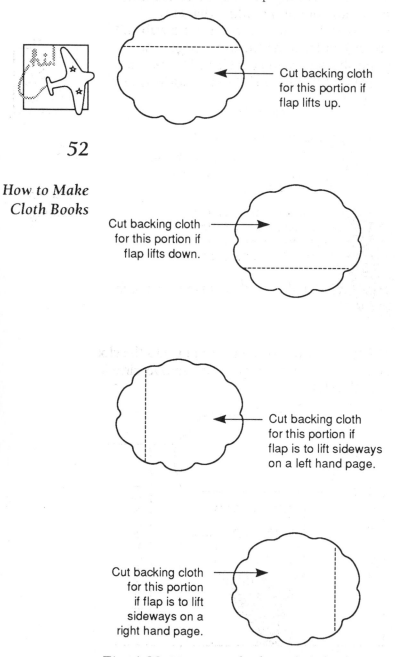

Cut backing cloth for this portion if flap lifts up.

Cut backing cloth for this portion if flap lifts down.

Cut backing cloth for this portion if flap is to lift sideways on a left hand page.

Cut backing cloth for this portion if flap is to lift sideways on a right hand page.

Fig. 4-32. How to cut backing cloth for flaps.

Carefully align the flap, with its fusible web backing and its fabric backing. Place it in the spot you wish to have it appear on the page. Remember, if the flap is to open sideways, always have the lift-up side farthest away from the folded edge of the page. This will allow the child to open the flap, rather than having it open automatically at the turning of the page. When you are sure you have it in the spot you want, cover with a damp press cloth and press at the recommended heat-setting for about 10 seconds.

When you take away the press cloth, quickly lift the flap while it is still warm, to test whether it bonded completely and can be lifted up easily.

You can make a tiny drawing under the flap with fabric crayons or paint. Be sure to set such designs with dry heat first, before you fuse the flap with the wet press cloth.

Making slots for photographs

You might prefer to slip photos in slots behind flaps. These slots are U-shaped pieces of fabric, bonded in such a way that the inner edge remains free. This allows you to slide in a photo. There are two ways to make the photo slots.

Method A: Purchase iron-on patches, or transform a piece of fabric into an iron-on piece by using paper-backed fusible web. Make sure it is a fabric with a very tight weave of many threads to the square inch, such as percale. Select white or a pale color that does not show through easily.

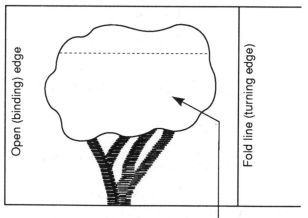

Open (binding) edge

Fold line (turning edge)

This part of tree is a lift-up flap with slot for photograph.

Fig. 4-33. Lift up Flap.

Measure the approximate space you will have hidden under each flap. Cut a small rectangle of the iron-on patch or the tightly woven fabric you have selected and backed with fusible web. Make this fabric rectangle just large enough to fit into the space under the flap.

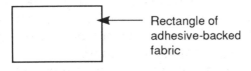

Fig. 4-34. *The first step in making a slot for photos.*

Test whether the rectangle is completely hidden when the flap is in place. It will save time if you can make all the flaps the same size, thereby allowing you to make the slots all the same size. However, that is not always feasible. In many cases, you must measure and cut each rectangle separately, matching it up to the particular space you have under a flap on that page.

Now cut away the center part of the rectangle, making a squared-off U shape with sides and bottom that are approximately 1/2" (1.3cm) wide. Using the U shape as a pattern, cut a second U shape of cotton fabric (without adhesive or fusible-web backing). Make this second U piece just large enough to cover the inner quarter-inch strip along the sides and bottom of your adhesive or fusible-web backed U shape.

Method A

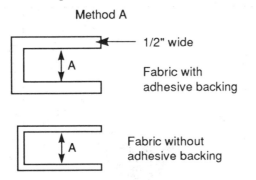

A is same distance in both.

Fig. 4-35. *The second step in making a slot for photos.*

Place the adhesive-backed U shape, with its smaller fabric U shape lined up carefully along the inner edges, in the exact spot you wish to have it appear on the page. Cover with a damp cloth and heat fuse.

Method B: If you want to decrease the amount of cutting needed, select a cotton cloth tape or seam binding that is 1/2" (1.3cm) wide. Back it with fusible web, 1/4" (6mm) wide, along the outer edge. The paper-backed hem tape (*Hem-N-Trim*) now made by Dritz in 1/4" (6mm) widths is ideal for this.

Method B

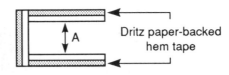

Three pieces of cloth tape or seam binding backed by Dritz paper-backed hem tape (1/4" wide along outer edges)

Fig. 4-36. *An alternate way to make a slot for photos.*

Cut the photo you wish to put into the slot so that it fits very snugly, but avoid forcing it into the slot.

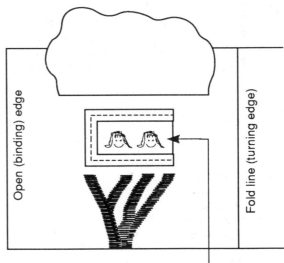

Photo slides in here.

Fig. 4-37. *Slide the photo into the slot under the flap.*

Fig. 4-38. Quien Va de Viaje?, *a Spanish-language picture book that involves lifting flaps to discover photos of children going on trips by different means of transportation.*

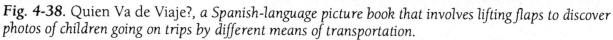

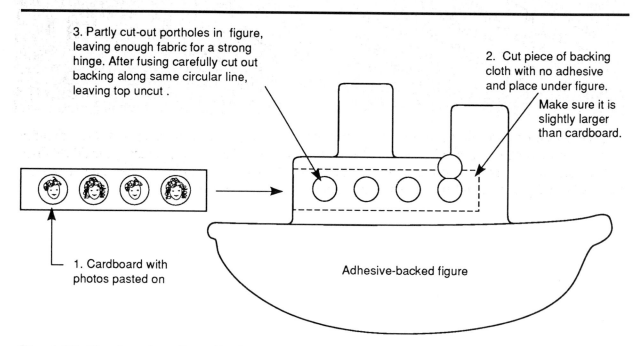

3. Partly cut-out portholes in figure, leaving enough fabric for a strong hinge. After fusing carefully cut out backing along same circular line, leaving top uncut.

2. Cut piece of backing cloth with no adhesive and place under figure.

Make sure it is slightly larger than cardboard.

1. Cardboard with photos pasted on

Adhesive-backed figure

Fig. 4-39. *How I made a photo slot for several photos on one piece of cardboard.*

Sometimes you might wish to have a row of flaps, in which case it is easier to paste the photos on a cardboard, and then slide the cardboard into a large slot that has been left free behind a part of your fused illustration. For the book *Quien Va de Viaje?* (Fig. 4-40) this technique was used to make photos appear behind portholes in a boat, and under window flaps in a bus.

First, I backed the entire bus and boat with paper-backed fusible web. I pulled away the paper backing. I made two cardboard rectangles just large enough to cover the line of bus windows and the line of boat portholes.

Then, I cut two rectangles of plain cotton fabric only a tiny bit larger than the cardboard rectangles. These rectangles of plain fabric were placed behind the bus window area and the boat portholes area between the figures and the background fabric, so that these areas would not fuse to the background page. Just before fusing the bus or boat to the page, I cut open a little of each bus window and each porthole. After the bus and boat were fused to the page, I completed cutting the portholes and windows, now with the cotton backing cloth fused to them, so that they made reinforced flaps (Fig. 4-39).

Fig. 4-40a and b. *Note that you can design such books in a way that allows the photos to be changed and used with another set of children. For the book* In Mrs. K's Classroom, *photos of the 20 children in the morning class can be easily pulled out and photos of the 20 children in the afternoon class put in. The following year, another two sets of child photos can be prepared.*

Objects

After you have made sure that no more ironing will be needed on a page, you can attach objects to the page, either openly or behind flaps. Select objects that are not too bulky. Small buttons of interesting shapes, plastic insects or other creatures that you can find in science museum shops, educational toy stores, or variety stores, and name tags are all ideal for hiding behind the flaps. Sew them on using thread the same color as the object. Be sure to attach them very well so that little children cannot take them off and swallow them.

Caution! Never use a detachable object in a book meant for very young children!

Fig. 4-41. Each page of In Grandpa's Garden *has fake insects, worms, or the like hidden among the flowers. They are very firmly sewn on.*

Tiny figures of machine-sewn appliqué are available in many craft and sewing-supply stores. These are also easy to sew or fuse onto the page, either beneath a flap or in open spots on the page. If you wish to let the child move these objects or figures around, attach a bit of *Velcro* or other hook-and-loop fastener to the back of the object. Place a corresponding bit of fastener on the pages where you wish the figure or object to rest. This is how I enabled Ellen to make the bumblebee fly, in the book I made for her called *The Flight of the Bumblebee.*

Fig. 4-42. *In* The Flight of the Bumblebee *the Velcro-backed bee can be moved from page to page. The book was made for Ellen at age three, when she was old enough to move the bee by herself. (The bee is upside-down here.)*

You can also put an object at the end of a string or elasticized thread and attach it to the upper left corner of the cover. By making a pocket for the object on the cover or front page, out of which the child can take the object, you allow both for manipulation and safekeeping of the object. An example of this is *Ananse Plays Hide and Seek*, created for a workshop in Ghana, West Africa.

Repeat caution! Never use a detachable object in a book meant for very young children!

Fig. 4-43. *Ananse the Spider is a favorite folk character in Ghana. Here he moves on the end of a string, to hide in a different spot on each page. When not in use, he rests inside a spider web on the front cover.*

Fig. 4-44. *Children enjoy filling pockets and manipulating buttons.*

Other kinds of manipulation that children enjoy include zipping zippers, buttoning buttons, buckling buckles, tying shoe laces, snapping shut large snaps, simple braiding and weaving, matching colors, matching shapes, opening curtains, looking in fake mirrors (created by using adhesive-backed silver Mylar on stiff cardboard), taking out tissues, and many more.

Method 7. Transferring photos to cloth

Children delight in seeing familiar sights in their books. You can use local scenes or family objects you've photographed.

Some commercial copy outlets will transfer photos to a T-shirt or similar article of clothing. You can use this process for a page or two, if it fits in with your design. For a book, however, you often need finer details from the photo than this process can pick up. Or, you might wish to have it in color, rather than black and white. You can do this several ways.

If you have access to a camera that takes slides and to a slide projector, you can pose the person or objects in just the way you want them on your page. Take the slide photo in horizontal format if you have horizontal pages; take it in vertical format if you have vertical pages.

Put the slide in a projector, and project it onto a wall. Tack or tape your cloth on the wall, in the spot where the projected photo falls. Move the projector backward or forward until you have it focused on the cloth in exactly the position you want. Remember to leave about 2" (5cm) unworked at the open (binding) edge. Trace the details you want directly on the cloth, with crayon or dressmaker pencil. Or if you prefer, trace the details onto a piece of paper the size of the page. You can then cut up the paper to make your patterns.

Cloth page or paper
the size of your page

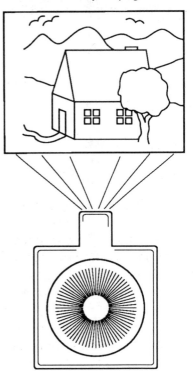

Fig. 4-45. Use a slide projector to help make images on paper or cloth.

If you have an existing photo that is not a slide, and have access to an overhead projector, you might be able to reduce or enlarge your photo to the page size you wish to use. This is a bit trickier, because the reduction

and/or enlargement is not as easy to manage as with a slide projector. Also, sometimes the image is not as sharp. First, you must trace the outlines of the photo onto a piece of clear acetate, using a *Sharpie* pen or similar type pen that writes clearly on acetate. Then, place the acetate on the overhead projector, and again tack or tape your cloth page or a piece of paper to the wall, where the projected image falls. Copy the details you want. This type of projector is available in most schools and libraries. Call ahead to schedule.

Cloth page or paper
the size of your page

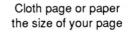

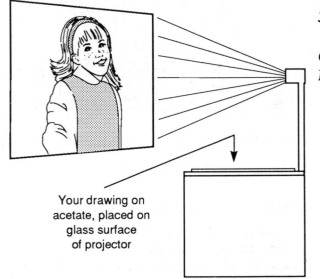

Your drawing on
acetate, placed on
glass surface
of projector

Fig. 4-46. To make a pattern from a photo, use an overhead projector.

The method used by the commercial copy outlets is the heat-transfer method. A photo is copied, enlarging it if necessary. Special heat-transfer paper is then placed over the photocopy and heated with an iron. This process lifts some of the ink from the photocopy onto the heat-transfer paper.

When the special paper is then placed over cloth and ironed according to the manufacturer's instructions, the image of the photo is transferred to the cloth. This special paper is available only in large art supply or craft stores. I have had mixed success in using it. Sometimes the photos have come out reasonably well. At other times they have ruined a page I was working on and I had to start again. There is also a liquid medium, such as *Picture This* or *Delta Transfer Photos to*

*Fig. 4-47. This photo of a corner in the Central
Children's Library, Accra, Ghana, was
photocopied and transferred to the cloth cover
using the medium Picture This.*

Fabric, that works in a similar manner but
does not require heat-setting. It, too, can
transfer only photos that have been photocopied, or printed pages from some magazines or newspapers.

Lettering the text

In most cases the exact text should be
worked out for each page in advance, on the
scrap-paper dummy. This will help to avoid
making mistakes in spelling, or in placement
on the page. I like to letter the text last, after
all the illustrations are in place. However, I
have worked with some parents who got so
excited about finishing a book for their
children within the time-frame of one workshop session, that they wanted to write down
the text as quickly as they finished the illustration for each page. If you are working with
such a group, it is important to recognize that
their spontaneity and enthusiasm, rather than
extensive planning and dummy-making, is
more likely to result in a book that is satisfy-
ing and appealing to them.

Choose a consistent style of writing and
stick to it for the entire book. There are two
basic types of writing: manuscript (uncon-
nected letters that look the same as printed
letters) and cursive (connected letters that
look like handwriting). Find out if the school
your child attends uses a particular style of
manuscript writing. Some Montessori schools
or other types of early childhood teaching
systems based on European methods like to
begin showing the child cursive writing from
early on. Others prefer that the child see
mainly manuscript printing.

Fig. 4-48. Two ways to write in your book.

Manuscript printing can be done with
whole circle style, partial circle style, or
connected style. In the whole circle style, the
rounded portions of letters are made with
whole circles. For example, the letter "d" is
made by first making a complete small circle,
"o" and then adding a straight long stroke at
the side: d . For the letter "g" a small complete circle "o" is followed by a down-stroke
line curving inward:

Fig. 4-49. Whole circle style.

In partial circle style, the letter "d" is made
by making only a partial circle "c", and then
adding the longer straight down stroke: d.

The letter "g" starts the same way, with a partial circle "c", and the down-stroke again curves inward at the bottom:

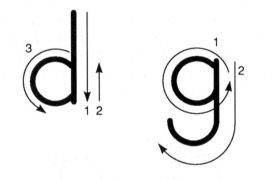

Fig. 4-50. *Partial circle style.*

Connected style in manuscript letters refers to connections within the letter, not connections from one letter to another. In connected style, the letter "d" is made without lifting the pen from the paper, by starting with the down stroke, then retracing over it a bit, upward, and completing the letter by making the half-circle on the left. The letter "g" in connected style begins with a circle, and then moves on to the down stroke, again, curving to the left.

Fig. 4-51. *Connected style.*

If you are not sure which type your child or children will be learning in school, just select the type that you are most comfortable with, and use it consistently throughout the book.

Decide what type of crayon, pen, or pencil you wish to use in writing the text. I personally like to use fabric crayons for texts of 15 or fewer words on each page, usually meant for little children. Not only can you choose a much broader range of colors, but they are much brighter than most fabric pens or pencils. Fabric pens or pencils are easier to use with longer texts, especially those for

older children who are ready to read them on their own.

Caution: If you are the type who is easily distracted into spelling mistakes, be sure to use crayons or pens of the fade-away type or the kind that can be washed out before they are heat-set. See pages 48 and 49 for fixing errors.

If you feel confident you can do the text without error, simply by following your dummy pages, then you might prefer to use fabric pens that set immediately and permanently, without heat. However, it is generally a good idea to do the text in a fade-away type of pen first, and then go over it with permanent pen or crayon.

You planned the text for your book when you made a dummy. Now you may want to practice lettering on paper the same size as your finished page before you letter the actual book. Select a piece of scrap paper about the size of your page and write the text for one page in ordinary pencil, in the approximate size and placement you think it should have.

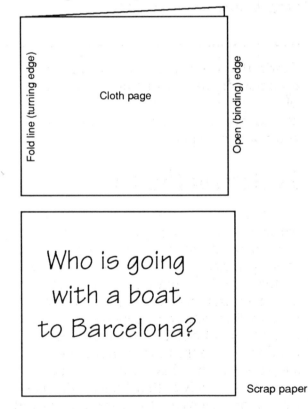

Fig. 4-52. *Practice your text on paper first.*

Note that you must not write too closely to the open edges of the pages because that space will be taken up by the binding. Also, watch out for long words. You should not hyphenate any words because children may not understand them. If a word will not fit well on the end space of a line, move it to the next line.

Do not be too fussy about printing perfectly straight and with all letters even and exactly the same size. You may resort to lettering stencils if you wish. But part of the charm of hand-made books is the fact that the lettering can have great individuality. If my letters turn out to be a little crooked and not quite in a straight line, I like to think of them as dancing across the page, just the way the children might if they were in the scene.

Avoid penciling in the text first with ordinary pencil, because it will invariably show through and take away from the aesthetics of the page. Avoid making lines on which to write your text. These will inevitably show and will suggest a school copy book rather than a book that is a pleasure to read and look at. If you really have trouble keeping to a reasonably straight line, place a paper with heavily marked lines under the cloth. In most cases, the line can be seen through the cloth well enough to be used as a guide. Or use a plastic, see-through ruler on the page as your guide.

I like to do the text last, after all the illustrations are in place. If you decide to place text in unusual positions in and around the illustrations, you might have to do some of the text at the same time as the illustrations. In such a case, remember to heat-set any text written with fabric crayon using **dry heat**. Generally, it is a good idea to do it before you do any fusing with the damp press cloth. Be sure to place paper towels **under and over** the text to be set with dry heat, and press until you are sure all of the excess crayon has been absorbed by the paper towel. Some fabric pens need no heat-setting at all. You can let them dry and they become permanent.

After you have each page of text lettered, either spread it out (if you have enough room) until all pages of text are completed; or heat-set each page immediately. Do not let the pages touch each other too much before you heat-set them, especially when using some types of fabric crayons. Tiny specks of crayon are likely to rub off onto the touching pages, and it is often hard to get them off before ironing.

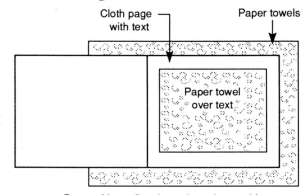

Press with medium heat, then change this upper paper towel and press again. Continue using paper towels until no crayon color comes off.

Fig. 4-53. *Heat-set text written with fabric crayons.*

62

How to Make Cloth Books

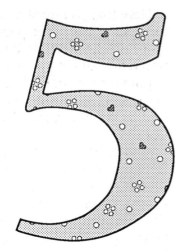

Finishing

Because Rachel and her sisters loved the Spot books by Eric Hill (published by Putnam), I made a personalized Spot book. Rachel learned to read in part by re-reading this book over and over again.

5

Finishing

❖ Step 1. Stiffening the pages
❖ Step 2. Finishing the page edges
❖ Step 3. Binding the pages into a book

64

*How to Make
Cloth Books*

*The final stage of getting the pages of
the book put together permanently
involves three parts:*

*1) The pages must be stiffened if
they are too limp for easy handling;*

2) The edges must be finished off;

*3) The pages must be bound in a
way that is appropriate for the child,
and that allows the book to be taken
apart for hand washing, if desired.*

Step 1.
Stiffening the pages

If your cloth is of medium weight, chances are the pages are not stiff enough to hold their shape easily. Clamp each set of pages together temporarily with large paper clamps. Then turn the pages one by one. If they seem limp, flop about, and destroy the effect of the illustrations, consider stiffening the pages in one of three ways: A) starching, B) interfacing, or C) using cardboard. When working with a group, check to make sure that each understands the cost, the benefits, and the ease or difficulty of assembling each type of stiffener. Starch and/or cardboard are the cheapest, but require a bit more work. Should your pages not need stiffening—for example, pages quilted back-to-back, skip this part and go directly to the section "Finishing the page edges" on page 66.

A) Starching the pages

If your pages are of mostly cotton fabric and are fairly stiff already, you might prefer to simply starch them, either with spray starch or with liquid starch. This will also give them a protective coating. You will not be able to use this technique if you have objects sewn on the pages that cannot tolerate a fairly high heat-setting when ironing. If using liquid starch, dip the pages carefully and hang them to drip dry by pinning the open edges on a line. When completely dry, press with an iron.

B) Interfacing as stiffening

The benefit of using interfacing is that it is washable and easiest to assemble. You will need one yard or meter of stiff, heavyweight interfacing for each book. If you are buying for a group, check how many participants need interfacing and buy accordingly. Some brand names are *Pellon* and *HTC Handler*. Some of these interfacings have a fusible web already bonded to one side and others do not. Select whichever type seems most appropriate for your pages.

Measure the size of your pages; subtract 1/4" (6mm) to 1/2" (1.3cm) from the height of the page. Subtract 1" (2.5cm) from the width of the page. This is the size your interfacing pages should be. Cut one page of interfacing for each folded pair of pages.

Place one piece of interfacing between the sides of the pair of folded pages, making sure there is equal space at the top and bottom (Fig. 5-2). Do not leave a space at the folded edge. Instead, line up the interfacing so that it comes right up to the inside of the folded edge. This should leave approximately 1" (2.5cm) of space on the open edge side and allow for binding without the extra bulk of the interfacing.

C) Cardboard as stiffener

If you prefer, you may use the cardboard found on the back of typewriter-size paper pads, or in discarded boxes. Cereal box cardboard is too lightweight and carton boxes are too thick. Remember that if you use cardboard, you will either not seal the side edges so that you can remove the cardboard for washing—or you plan to never wet the book. Locate enough cardboard so that you can cut pieces to fit between all of the pages. To determine the size of cardboard needed, subtract a full 1/2" (1.3cm) from the height of your cloth page and 1" (2.5cm) from the width of your page.

Put the cardboard aside until you have finished off the top and bottom edges of the pages.

Fig. 5-1. The Ananse book is stiffened with cardboard.

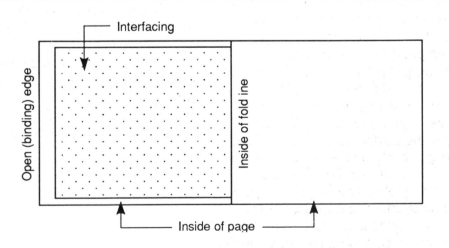

Fig. 5-2. Place interfacing inside the folded pair of pages.

Step 2.
Finishing the page edges

The folded pages must be sealed at the top and bottom edges (or the side edges if you have a book that opens "up" instead of sideways). You also have to decide whether or not to close the open edge. All the edges can be sealed and finished off by A) sewing, B) using strips of fusible web, or C) using iron-on seam binding. Open edges can be cut with pinking shears. Sealing the top and bottom prevents the stiffening from falling out or getting crooked. Even if you are not using stiffening, the folded pages will hold their shape much better if they are sealed at the top and bottom. Also, sealed edges give the book a more finished look.

A) Sewing the edges

First, decide if you wish to leave your open edges at the side unseamed. Many fabrics look quite all right with the side edges pinked, and need no seams at all. Others need a more finished look because they ravel easily. If you wish, turn under each open edge approximately 1/2" (1.3cm) and sew each edge separately. If you prefer, you may also fuse them under separately (Fig. 5-3).

The top and bottom edges can be sewn on the inside (making an invisible seam) or on the outside. If you wish to have an invisible seam, turn the folded pages inside out, right sides together, and sew a seam at top and bottom, about 1/2" (1.3cm) from the edge. Make sure you are not going to sew over any part of text or illustrations. Start at the open (binding) edge, sew to the folded (turning) edge, turn the fabric around, and sew back over or parallel to the original seam, returning to the open edge where you started. This creates a strong seam.

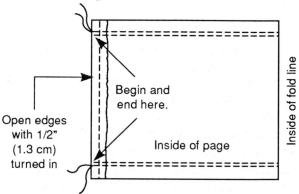

Fig. 5-4. To sew pages invisibly, turn pages inside out and sew top and bottom edges.

Turn the page to the outside, push out the corners with the end of your scissors or one of the special tools made for this, and then press the upper and lower edges. Slide in

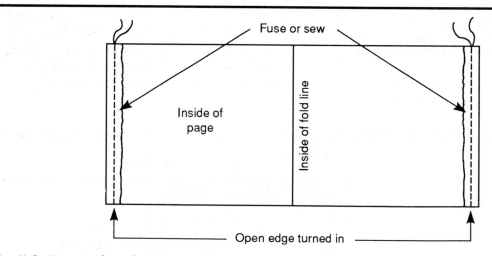

Fig. 5-3. Turn in the side edges and fuse or sew.

cardboard or other stiffener, if you are using them. No stiffener should be in the binding area.

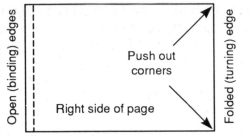

Fig. 5-5. *Turn page right side out and push out corners.*

You might prefer to sew a visible seam on the outside, perhaps in a contrasting color. In this case, simply line up your folded-over edge carefully, with the right sides out, wrong sides together. Begin at the open edges, sew to the folded edge, turn the fabric around, and continue sewing parallel to the original seam until you come back to the point you started at, near the open edge. Sew both top and bottom edges in this manner. Be sure that as you sew, you also attach the interfacing, if any.

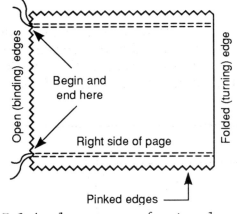

Fig. 5-6. *An alternate way of sewing edges.*

If you wish, sew seam binding, ribbon, or other strips of cloth around the edges. However, it takes considerable sewing skill to get the binding and the seams exactly even on both sides of the page.

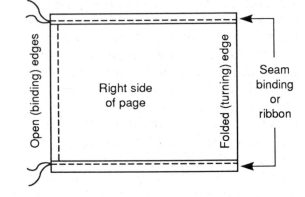

Fig. 5-7. *You can also bind edges.*

B) Fusing the edges

If you prefer, use plain fusible web to seal the edges. Either roll up the fusible web jelly-roll fashion and cut strips that are approximately 1/2" (1.3cm) wide, or use the pre-cut narrow rolls of fusible web recommended for hemming. (You can also use strips of paper-backed fusible web. It takes an extra step to fuse, remove paper, fuse.)

If you have used interfacing, open up the pair of folded pages, place a fusible web strip so that it is lying half on the interfacing and half on the bottom cloth page. Do this on both upper and lower edges of the page. Carefully fold the top page over again, making sure to align the top and bottom edges. Check to see that no fusible web is sticking out. If using starch or interfacing stiffener, you can also fuse together the side edges (Fig. 5-8).

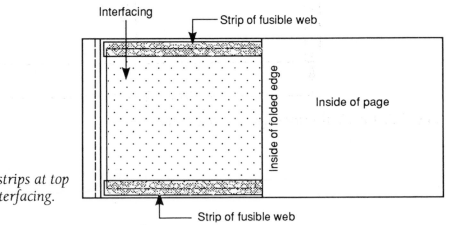

Fig. 5-8. *Place fusible web strips at top and bottom, half over the interfacing.*

Fig. 5-9. *This "Quiet Book," made by Sinsinawa Handcraft has pages edged with decorative machine stitching in a loose zigzag pattern. This group is no longer in business.*

Using a damp strip of cloth, heat-set the upper and lower edges of the pages with an iron. Take care not to touch any parts of illustrations made of heat-sensitive materials.

If you have cardboard stiffeners and wish to fuse the top and bottom edges instead of sewing them, put the cardboards aside. Place the fusible web strips in as straight a line as possible, as close to the top and bottom page edges as possible. Heat-set as above. Take care not to touch any parts of illustrations made of heat-sensitive materials. When the edges are cool, slide in the cardboards. You may have to trim them a bit, but do not over-trim. They should fit snugly inside the pages. You can then fuse the side edges but will not be able to remove the cardboard and thus cannot wash the book.

C) Iron-on seam binding

Many fabric stores carry iron-on seam binding in 3-yd. (2.75m) packets. If you like the look of a border of contrasting color, you can fuse such seam binding on the top and bottom edges of each of your pages. You might even prefer to do it on the open side edge if you used interfacing stiffener. If you cannot find the color you want in the iron-on type of seam binding, look for the color you want in regular seam binding or cloth ribbon. Then transform that seam binding or ribbon into the iron-on type by using paper-backed fusible web in 1/2" (1.3cm) width.

Edging single thickness pages

If you used single thickness pages of canvas or other heavy fabric, you should finish off at least the right edge (the turning edge) of each page. Do this with iron-on seam binding or fused binding or ribbon, or by sewing with special edging stitches such as can be found on many newer machines. It will look better if you can finish off all three sides.

Step 3.
Binding the pages into a book

You can bind your cloth book in many ways. The type of binding you choose should depend not only on your skills, but on the age of the child for whom you have made the book. A) For little children, a sturdily sewn or fused binding is best. However, books bound in this manner are harder to take apart to repair or to wash individual pages. B) Punched holes, or C) sewn buttonholes secured with brightly colored shoelaces, are very attractive and make a book that is easy to take apart. An unusual and very finished effect can be achieved with wooden or leather toggle buttons and large buttonholes or loops. For books that will get a lot of handling by many children, metal grommets, ring binder fasteners or similar methods are appropriate. This book describes only a few basic methods. You may wish to experiment with your own type of binding.

Fig. 5-10. Four examples showing the two easiest types of binding to make: A) Sewing and fusing (first and third from left) and B) Punched holes (second and fourth from left).

A) Sewing and fusing

Stack and line up all the pages in correct order. Trim any left edges that are out of line. For hand sewing, use a large needle and good quality cotton thread. If you have a machine capable of sewing through many thicknesses, use a size 100(16) jeans needle with a sharp point and polyester thread. Sew a seam through all of the pages 1/2" (1.3cm) from the open edges on the left side. Sew a parallel return seam to give added strength.

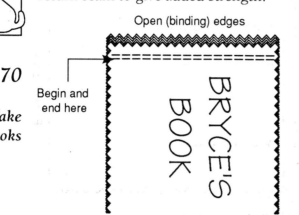

Fig. 5-11. *Stack pages and sew, using a sturdy needle.*

After finishing the seam, put a secure knot in the ends of the threads. Open the book and page through it to check that you have caught all of the open edges. Occasionally, an edge can slip out of place while you are in the process of sewing all the thicknesses. To insert this loose page, it is best to take out your stitches and redo the seam completely.

Once you are sure all the pages are secure, cut a strip of fabric in a color that matches or contrasts with your cover. It should be about 1-1/2" – 2" (4cm – 5cm) wide, and as high as the book. If possible, cut so that a selvage falls along one of the long sides of the strip. (The selvage is the strong, thickly woven edge of the fabric that prevents it from ravelling.) Then cut two narrow strips of fusible web, each about 1/2" (1.3cm) wide and as high as the book.

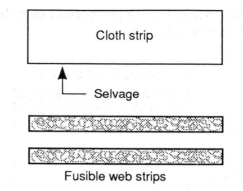

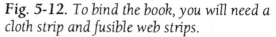

Fig. 5-12. *To bind the book, you will need a cloth strip and fusible web strips.*

Place one strip of fusible web under the selvage of the fabric strip, line them both up along the sewn seam on the front of the book, so that they just hide the stitches of the seam. Place a damp strip of cotton pressing cloth over the strip, and heat-set with your iron. Let the edge cool.

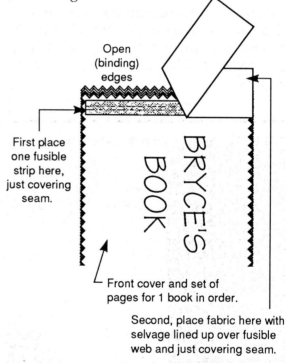

Fig. 5-13. *Binding is a two-step process.*

Turn the book over. Place the other strip of fusible web along the back of the seam. Stretch the fabric taut and turn it under (about 1/4" [6cm]) along the entire strip. Try to make it come out so that the outer edge of the fusible web and the turned-under edge of the fabric strip line up exactly, just covering the sewn seam. Place a damp cloth over the fabric strip and heat-fuse.

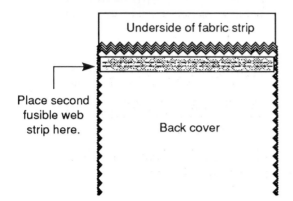

Fig. 5-14. *Finish binding on the back cover.*

You now have a bound book.

B) Punched holes

This is also an easy method of binding. It works well with cardboard stiffeners because if one of the pages become damaged or wet, it is easy to replace the cardboard. Measure the left open edge and divide the space into five equal segments. Note where the four dividing points fall.

Mark each page at these same four spots along the open edges. Place the spots 1/2" (1.3cm) from the edge (if you have turned under your edges) or 3/4" (2cm) from the edge (if you have not turned then under).

With a sharp paper punch, punch a hole through the cloth at each of the spots. Use the type of punch that makes a small hole, not a large one.

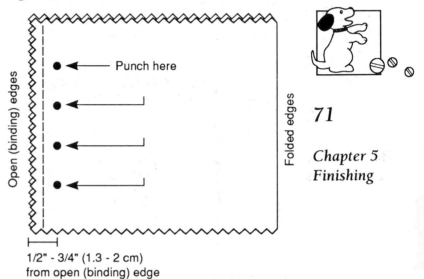

Open (binding) edges

Folded edges

Punch here

1/2" - 3/4" (1.3 - 2 cm)
from open (binding) edge

Fig. 5-16. *Punch four holes.*

Fig. 5-15. *The finished bound book.*

When you have punched holes in all of the pages, stack the pages in order. Then string a colorful shoelace (28" [71cm] length) through the holes in the following manner:

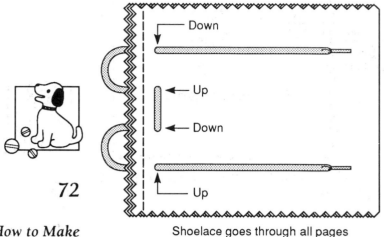

Fig. 5-17. String with a shoelace, starting at the top front hole.

Make sure you end up with approximately equal lengths of shoelace on the cover of the book. Tie the ends into a knot, and then into a bow.

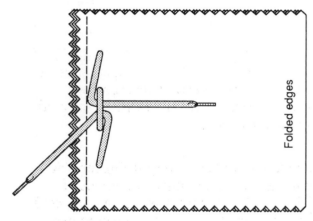

Fig. 5-18. Tie ends with a knot, then with a bow.

C) Sewn buttonholes

If you have a buttonhole attachment for your machine and enjoy sewing buttonholes, make buttonholes for the binding and show off your skills. Measure the open edge of your cover page and divide into three segments. If you have doubled the edges inward, mark the

two dividing points 1/2" (1.3cm) from the edge; if you have not turned them under, mark the points 3/4" (2cm) from the edge.

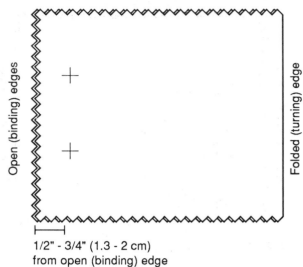

Fig. 5-19. Mark the places for buttonholes.

Make 1/4" (6cm)-long vertical buttonholes at each of these two points. If you are going to use cardboard as stiffener, you will have to make four buttonholes, two each on the

Fig. 5-20. I bind many books with shoelaces because it's easy to take them apart for cleaning.

upper fabric and two each on the lower fabric, so you can slide the cardboard out to wash the book.

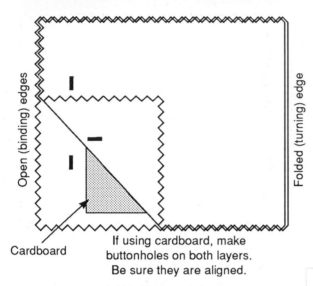

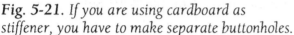

Fig. 5-21. *If you are using cardboard as stiffener, you have to make separate buttonholes.*

When you have all the buttonholes complete, string a shoelace, colorful cord, or ribbon through the holes, and tie in front in a bow.

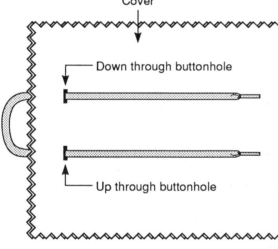

Fig. 5-22. *String with a shoelace, starting at the top front hole.*

Toggle buttons
If you wish to use toggle buttons, make the buttonholes longer. Make sure they are just long enough to allow you to pass the toggle button through. Do not make buttonholes on the last page. Instead, attach the two toggle buttons at the two points, making sure you leave enough thread or fastening tape between the button and the point where you are fastening it to the page to include all the

pages. This shank will allow you enough room to "button on" each page in order.

Fig. 5-23. *Toggle buttons turn perpendicular to the buttonholes.*

Fig. 5-24. *Toggle buttons make this book easy to take apart. Because many of the pages have unusual textures to feel, it is likely they will need repair now and then.*

If you wish to have a very strong binding that holds up to handling by hundreds of children (as in a school, hospital, library, etc.) you might wish to consider metal grommets and a three-ring binder type of holder, as in Marla Ostrowski's version of *My Quiet Book*.

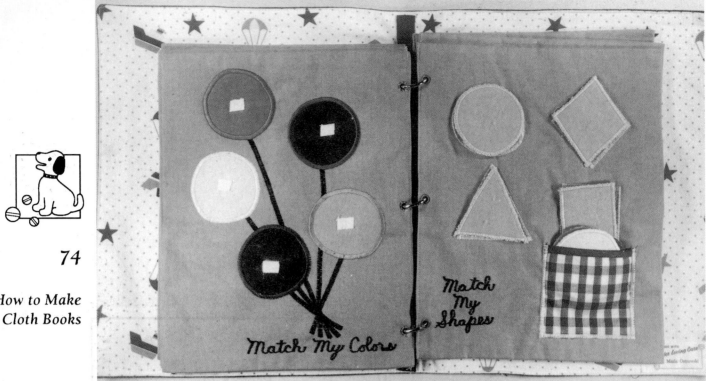

Fig. 5-25. *In binding her versions of* My Quiet Book, *Marla Ostrowski uses metal grommets and a three ring binder holder. Her sewn books are meant to stand up to years of use by hundreds of children.*

To do this, you will need to purchase the grommets, and to borrow or purchase the device to attach them to cloth.

Begin again!

I hope the many examples of books shown here will inspire you to make many cloth books. Once you have made one, share it with a child or children special to you. The mutual delight will make you want to start another book immediately.

I would like to hear about your efforts and would be pleased to see a photo of a page or two of which you are particularly proud. Write to me in care of Open Chain Publishing, Inc., (P.O. Box 2634-B, Menlo Park, CA 94026). (Enclose a stamped, self-addressed envelope if you want the photo returned.)

Should you wish to have information about group workshops or classes in cloth book-making, please write me in care of Open Chain Publishing.

Heidi's Bedtime Book. Another version of the "bedtime book" idea. The quilt is of the same material as Heidi's actual quilt. It can be lifted up and is kept in place by small Velcro tabs.

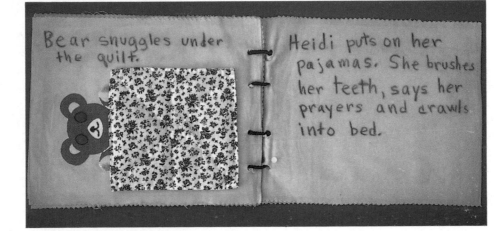

Children love the idea of finding a photo of themselves behind the windows or doors of a bus, train, plane, car, or boat.

On Saturday, April
looked in the poppies.
She saw a bump on the stem.
"It is a cocoon," said Mommy.
"The caterpillar is resting
inside."
April watched and waited.

The three versions I made
of this garden book were
helped by the fact that
beautiful floral prints are
relatively easy to find.

The final page of *Let's Go Fishing*
allows Aaron to discover a big
worm.

Cover of book shown on page 43.

In Mrs. K's Classroom serves as an introduction to the places and things children will encounter when they enter this pre-school.

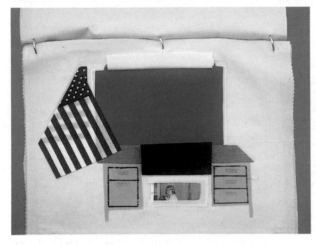

Because the white clouds were already printed on this blue fabric, it was very easy make a flap book, using the techniques described in Chapter 4. The six words are: "Happy Birthday to April Diane Beck."

Jane Genzel, a student in my class at University of Wisconsin-Milwaukee, made this picture book version of the Ojibway creation myth. The page edges are not finished yet. They will probably be sewn to suggest leather thong bindings.

In the rain forest
parrots chatter to
each other.
But where is
the black cat?

In The

Rain

Forest

In the Rain Forest was designed for children to have fun while learning a bit of visual discrimination. The bright colors and many details in the printed fabric are especially attractive.

In the rain forest
the toucans eat flower
seeds and nuts.
But where is
the black cat?

The Flight of the Bumblebee
a book for Ellen

from Aunt Anne

The bumble bee moves from page to page, finding different family members. This book is described in greater detail on page 56.

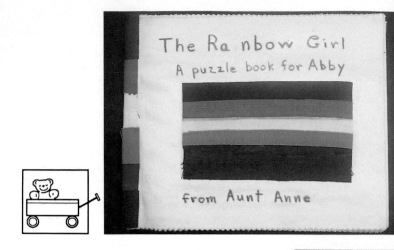

Abby loves rainbows, so I created this puzzle book for her. Each page features articles of a different color, and the last page brings together all of the colors.

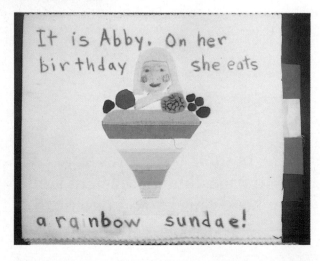

On the last page, all the different colors of the rainbow are in Abby's rainbow sundae.

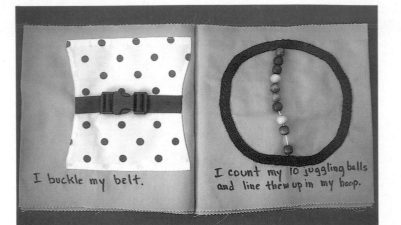

This variant of a "quiet" book was inspired by my nephew-in-law, an amateur clown who often performs for children.

Page from *Au Au Lambau*, one of a series of hand-sewn books from Brazil, each one involving a "transformation." In this case, how reading books can "transform" one's life.

I saw two manta rays using the ball to toss a game of catch.

Swimming in and out, seven slippery eels slid the ball through the seaweed.

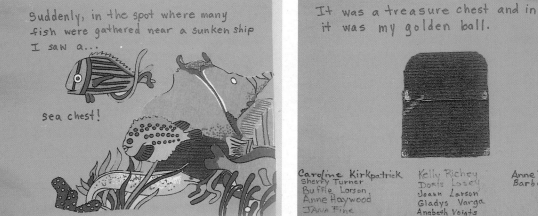

Suddenly, in the spot where many fish were gathered near a sunken ship I saw a...

sea chest!

It was a treasure chest and in it was my golden ball.

Caroline Kirkpatrick
Sherry Turner
Buffie Larson
Anne Haywood
JAwa Fine

Kelly Richey
Doris Losey
Joann Larson
Gladys Varga
Anabeth Voigts

Anne Page.
Barbara Rixey

This Catfish Calhoun fabric print of tropical fishes was used to make *Under Tampa Bay*. The fabric was so attractive, I bought yards and yards of it and used it for workshops in Venezuela, Egypt, Ghana, and Germany, as well as in many places throughout the U. S.

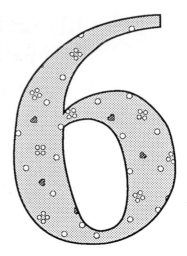

Bibliography

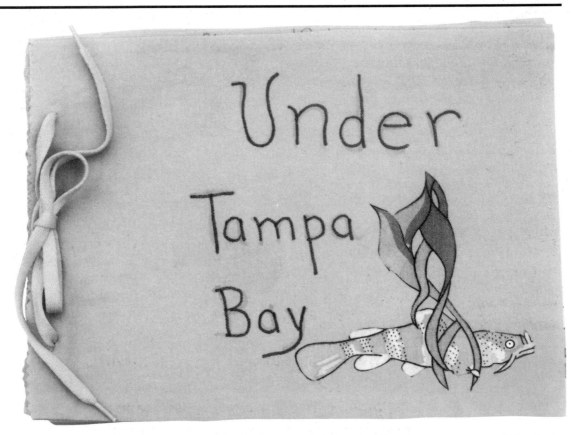

A group of librarians and teachers in Tampa, Florida made this during a library workshop, before working on their individual books. I often start off a workshop with such a group effort, so as to demonstrate some of the basic techniques of making cloth books. The group book is then given to the library.

A brief history and bibliography related to cloth books for children

Old cultures

Drawing or painting sequential pictures on cloth is a very old custom in some cultures. In India, many variants of the stories found in such ancient texts as the Ramayana, the Mahabharata, and the Panchatantra have been pictured on cloth, and then shown while a narrator tells or chants the tale in words, sometimes accompanied by music. This has been going on for at least two thousand years. In a sense, these were among our earliest picture books, and parts of them were probably appreciated as much by children as by adults.

Other Asian, African and Native American groups have used colored cloth as the basis of arts or crafts that have also had the same or similar functions as a picture book. For example, among certain Hmong groups today, one can find artisans making cloth constructions that include sequential pictures (and often text) that tell a story. There are evidences of a similar custom surviving in such far apart cultures as that of Benin in West Africa, Chile in South America, and the Kuna people living off the coast of Panama in Central America. The *kanga* cloths used in many areas of East Africa traditionally have had pictures and a Swahili proverb or saying printed on the cloth. Currently, a group in Kenya is working out a means to have the *kanga* also serve as a child's picture book.

All of the above mentioned forms of visual expression through cloth can be considered related to the child's first picture books. They might even have an influence on how the child's picture book is perceived in any given culture. The fact that cloth is so much more tactile than paper can perhaps explain in part why cloth books are so appealing to young children.

The modern picture book

The modern picture book for children does not have a long history. Generally, these books were and are printed on paper, and because they were appealing to children, many were literally used up. Nevertheless, enough books survived so that we can see examples of early printed picture books for children in quite a number of public and private collections, and there are a number of histories written about them. There are also a few surviving examples of the use of cloth in early children's books.

Some public and private collections contain one or more of the "Drawing Room Dress Books" produced by the firm of E. C. Bennett in London in the mid-nineteenth century. In these books, the central character in each illustrated page wore clothing, especially skirts, made of actual cloth, that could be fluffed up and made to stand out from the page.

Rag books

Very few of the histories of books for children, however, refer specifically to cloth books. Barbara Bader devoted about five pages to this type of book in her *American Picturebooks From Noah's Ark to the Beast Within* (Macmillan, 1976). But only books produced in the U. S. are referred to there.

Iona Opie, in her text for Part Two of *The Treasures of Childhood* (Arcade Publishing, 1989) makes the statement that the British publisher, Dean, invented the term "rag book," probably around the year 1905, since the patent was applied for in March of that year. They issued their first titles in the "Rag Book Series" at the same time. Prior to that, according to Opie, there had been some cloth books for children, but the illustrations and text were printed on paper which was then glued to the cloth. Among the first titles issued by Dean in the "Rag Book Series" were:

The Three Bears
Big Animal Rag Book
Bow-wow's Rag Book
Mother Goose's Rag Book
Nursery Rhyme Rag Book

Later, Dean issued titles under other series, such as *Fluffidown Rag Books*. Within a few years, many of their rag books were issued in French, German, Dutch, Swedish, Hungarian and other languages under agreements with publishers on the continent. Dean, which is now a division of the Hamlyn/Reed group, continues to publish cloth books for children.

Linen books

According to Brian Aldersen, other nineteenth century British publishers who produced books mounted on linen were Griffith & Farran, George Routledge, and Frederick Warne. This last-named publisher later produced *Everlasting Nursery Gift Books* which were printed directly on cloth, but there is no date indicated.

However, it is possible that McLoughlin Brothers Publishers of New York had published picture books for children, printed on linen, long before 1906. In a McLoughlin advertisement on the back of several of their books dated 1878 is the statement: "Any of these books (priced at \$.25 and printed on paper) can be had Mounted on Linen, price sixty cents each." But starting in the 1880's they seem to have taken to printing a number of books directly on linen, among them:

> *The ABC of Nature*, c. 1884
> *Jack and the Beanstalk*, illus. by R. Andre, c. 1888
> *Cinderella* (Aunt Friendly's Colored Picture Books), c. 188x
> *Baby Bunting ABC*, c. 1899
> *Domestic Animals*, c. 1900
> *A Birthday Treat and Other Stories*, c. 1902
> *Ding-Dong Bell*, c. 1905

Since virtually all of these books were printed on paper as well, using the same illustrations, it is impossible to say definitively just when they began printing directly on linen, because the publisher could well have used the same plates (with the same copyright notice) on early paper editions and then on cloth editions of a later date.

Many well-known illustrators of the 19th century designed cloth books for McLoughlin. Among them were Thomas Nast, Ida Waugh and William Momberger. It was probably the Santa Claus books illustrated by Thomas Nast for McLoughlin, as much as his magazine illustrations, that defined the image of Santa that would remain much the same up to the present day.

Muslin books

The Saalfield Publishing Company, based in Akron, Ohio, began publishing its series of *Saalfield Muslin Books* in 1906. Whether they were directly imitating the Dean rag books or the McLoughlin Brothers books is not entirely clear. The first Saalfield Muslin Books were issued in four series, with four titles in each series. The titles were:

Series 1, 12 pages each, 4-1/2" by 6" (11.5cm by 15cm), \$.15 each

> *Mother Goose Favorites*
> *Baby's Toys*
> *Tiny Tot's ABC Book*
> *Baby's Pets*

Series 2, 12 pages each, 6" by 9" (15cm by 23cm), \$.25 each

> *On the Nursery Stairs*
> *Nursery Pets*
> *Furry Friends*
> *My Playmates' ABC*

Series 3, 16 pages each, 8" by 9", \$.50 each

> *Who Killed Cock Robin?*
> *My ABC Book*
> *Baby's Friends*
> *Baby's Doings*

Series 4, 18 pages each, 8" by 11-1/2" (20.5cm by 29.5cm), \$.75 each

> *The Night Before Christmas*
> *Baby's ABC Book*
> *Mother Goose Jingles*
> *Animal Book*

A few new series were added each year. In 1908, Muslin Cut-Out Books were introduced. These were in interesting shapes. The first four titles in that series included *Dolly's Sewing Bee*, *Baby's Home Pets*, *Baby's Menagerie* and *Babies of All Nations*. By 1916, there were 30 series in all, most of them with four titles in each series.

In looking at the illustrations, you can see that a number of them were repeated in whole or in part in different combinations in the individual books. In most cases, the illustrator's name is not mentioned. There are a few exceptions. Mrs. Percy Wright is credited with the drawings modeled on the work of Kate Greenaway. Virginia Albert is cited as the illustrator for some of the more popular titles.

Cloth books from publishers

Saalfield Publishing Company and McLoughlin Brothers Pub. Co. seem to have had a corner on the cloth book market in the United States until the appearance of the trade-marked *Linenette Books* of Gabriel Publishing Company (first one issued in 1928?); the *Playroom Rag Books* of Harper Publishers (first one issued in 1930); a few cloth book titles published by William F. Scott Publishers (first one issued in 1938); the *Cloth Books* of Holiday House Publishers (first one issued in 1939); the self-published silk-screened picture books of Eleska (first one issued in 1941); and the *Peggy Cloth Books* (first one issued in 1945). Most of these cloth books do not appear in the Cumulative Book Index, so they are very difficult to trace. A number of them appear never to have been copyrighted.

The following list of several important titles in each of the above series was compiled mostly from advertisements on the back of one or more of the books in each series, or from advertisements or announcements in *Publisher's Weekly*:

Linenette Books, Samuel Gabriel Sons Publishers
 Four-footed Friends, no date
 Book of Trains, no date
 Farmyard Friends, no date
 Mother Goose, no date
 Friends at the Zoo, no date
 The Three Bears, no date
 The Night Before Christmas, no date
 The Little Red Hen, no date

Playroom Rag Books, Harper Publishers
 Chicken Little; illus. by Jimmy Garthwaite, c. 1930
 Sing a Song of Sixpence; illus. by Lois Lenski, c. 1930
 Sounds Pretty; illus. by Dan Web, c. 1948

William R. Scott Publishers (no series title)
 Cottontails; illus. by Sister Mary Veronica Scott, c. 1938
 Our Day; illus. by Mary Dana, c. 1940
 The Jingle Book; illus. by Mary Dana, c. 1940

Cloth Book Series, Holiday House Publishers
 No. 1, (Objects) illus. by Leonard Weisgard, c. 1939
 No. 2, (Zoo Animals) illus. by Glen Rounds, c. 1939
 No. 3, (Vehicles) illus. by Leonard Weisgard, c. 1940
 No. 4, (Food) illus. by Glen Rounds, c. 1940
 No. 5, (Familiar Activities) illus. by Leonard Weisgard, c. 1941
 No. 6, (Farm Animals) illus. by Kurt Wiese, c. 1942

Designed and published by Eleska; each book has 6 or 8 leaves.
 I See, 1941
 I Count, 1941
 I Eat, 1943
 I Play, 1944
 I Hear, no date given; first listed in 1947 advertisement
 Papa, Mama, Baby, no date given; first listed in 1947 (later issued as *I Love*)
 Our Neighbors, 1944

Peggy Cloth Books, New York; each book has 6 leaves

Peggy Cloth Books, New York; each book has 6 leaves

   Let's See the ABC, c.1945
   Let's Be Friends, c.1946
   Baby's Mother Goose, c.1947
   Oh, Look!, c.1948

This designer seems to have been the first to produce books with a tiny doll or animal character on the end of a string attached to the upper left binding of the book. The doll or character could then be moved from page to page.

Some of the above books were printed on special presses by companies such as Printex Corporation. Others, like many of the Eleska books, were individually silk-screened by hand.

More recently, the publisher Random House has specialized in various series of cloth books for children. According to Gina Abend, currently managing director of their Books for Young Readers, Random House began printing cloth books in approximately 1979. About 33 titles have been produced since that time. Some of these titles, such as *The Cow Says Moo*, have sold over half a million copies.

Handmade cloth books

The handmade cloth books are particularly difficult to locate today, since they were made in much smaller quantities than books printed on cloth or paper. Some were commercially sold only within very limited geographical areas. This is especially true of various versions of the cloth books known generally as "Quiet Books" or "Busy Books." It has proven impossible so far to track down the first use of these terms to refer to cloth books that involve such activities as buttoning, tying shoelaces, zipping zippers, etc.

Most of the handmade cloth books dating to the period 1930-1970 were alphabet books, nursery rhyme books or amusing animal picture books. Many were hand-embroidered and/or appliquéd, and they were usually personalized for a specific child by the use of a name, initials, or some other reference. Frieda Riggs of Bronxville, New York remembers being taught (in the 1940's)

how to make cloth books by an arts and crafts teacher from Kentucky, Mary Allen Tippett. Mrs. Riggs used the skills she acquired to make books for her children and grandchildren. Most of them were based on events that happened in the lives of these specific children.

The earliest handmade cloth book that I have been able to locate in the United States is a book made circa 1910, consisting of 12 folded-over pages (24 sides) of dark green cotton, onto which are pasted pictures cut from magazines, seed catalogs, children's clothing catalogs, etc. It was made for the mother of Kathy Carlisle of Selma, Oregon. Doris Hall of Rockville, Maryland owns a similar type, made for her by her grandmother in the 1920's.

Outline embroidery patterns were used for some handmade books, generally showing nursery rhyme characters or other well-known fictional characters. Mrs. John Bucklin of California has a good example of this type, made for her in 1931 by her grandmother.

A number of adaptations of the "Quiet Book" idea are currently available through specialized commercial outlets. Direct mail catalog outlets such as Lillian Vernon have sometimes commissioned the production of such books in other countries. Many are variants of the "Quiet Book" idea, with pages on which the child can manipulate something. Some of these books are made in China where cotton cloth and hand labor are comparatively lower in cost. Other variants are made by individuals who design them to order. See the list appearing in the previous section.

International cloth books

Cloth books for children have appeared in other countries as well. In France, the beautiful Bible story book, *La Plus Vieille Histoire du Monde*, with illustrations by Françoise Seignebosc, was introduced in a special promotion (along with the first Babar book) by Le Jardin des Modes in 1931.

For the World's Fair in 1958 in Brussels, the illustrator Helga Aichinger created a special edition of *Der Rattenfänger* (Pied Piper of Hamelin) that was printed on linen by Hugo Seifert, Linz, Austria in the *Werkstätten der Kunstschule* (Workshops of the Art School). This 12-sided linen fold-up book had one side clear, meant for children to draw on.

In Japan, the Coordinating Committee for Promotion of Cloth Picture Books brought together a wide range of volunteer groups (mostly of women) who designed and made cloth books for children with special needs. In 1978 and 1979 they organized a very large exhibition of more than 400 titles of such handmade books. They published a booklet explaining their philosophy and depicting (in photographs) some of the resulting books and their uses. This booklet, *The Future of Cloth and Tactile Picture Books*, was published by Kaisei-sha Publishing Company in 1980, and in a revised edition in 1985 (see Fig. 1-5, page 9). The Committee continues to function, and many of the groups continue to produce more and more handmade books for children with special needs.

Individuals and groups in Denmark, Norway and Sweden also participated in that exhibition, and a few of them (for example, the group affiliated with a Danish School for Special Education) have continued to make cloth books for children with special needs. Some of those items can be seen at the IBBY Documentation Centre on Books for and About Handicapped Children, c/o Norwegian Postgraduate College for Special Education, Granasen 4, Hosle 1347, Norway.

Annette Diesen is perhaps the best-known of the designers from Nordic countries who have experimented with commercially made cloth books for special children. A list of those titles can be found in the section, "Bibliography Related to Books for Special Children" on page 82.

In Brazil, the editor, Isis Valeria Gomes, working with a group of writers and illustrators of children's books, designed several ingenious cloth books, each one involving a transformation of some sort. These cloth

Fig. 6-1. *The print fabrics produced under the trade name Catfish Calhoun are often ideal for cloth books. How the Monkey Went Bananas was created entirely from one yard of a Catfish Calhoun print.*

books are produced by women's cooperatives, who use them as a means of earning cash income; the sale of the books benefits an unusual children's library and cultural center in a "favela" in Rio de Janeiro, Espaco Vivo. *Au Au Lambau* is one of the titles produced in that series. These ingenious books are marketed through a special department of Melhoramentos Publishers in Sao Paulo, Brazil.

Cloth books for children, both the printed variety, the hand-screen types, and the hand-sewn kinds are relatively rare. Few can be found in library or museum collections. Most of them are in the hands of private collectors. And there are virtually no check-lists of titles or historical studies that describe in detail the many unusual types of cloth books for children that have appeared over the years. This is an aspect of the history of children's books that remains to be researched more thoroughly.

Bibliography

Aldersen, Brian. "Rag Books." Typescript manuscript, 1991.

Bader, Barbara. *American Picturebooks from Noah's Ark to the Beast Within.* Macmillan, 1976.

Books for Disabled Young People. IBBY Documentation Center, Oslo, Norway, 1991.

Brown, Louise Fargo. "Eleska." *Horn Book,* 21: 337-343 (Sept. 1945).

"Cloth Books by Eleska Studios." *Publisher's Weekly,* 1696-7 (April 29, 1944).

The Future of Cloth and Tactile Picture Books, compiled by the Co-ordinating Committee for the Promotion of Cloth Picture Books. Kaisei-sha, Tokyo, Japan, 1981. Revised and reprinted, 1985.

Haining, Peter. *Movable Books.* New English Library, 1979.

Hogarth, Grace Allen. "Toy, Play and Game Books for Indoor Days." *Horn Book,* 19: 21-26 (Jan. 1943).

Mair, Victor H. *Painting and Performance;* *Chinese Picture Recitation and Its Indian Genesis.* University of Hawaii Press, 1988.

One Hundred Years of Children's Books. McLaughlin Brothers Publishers, 1928.

Opie, Iona and Robert and Brian Alderson. *The Treasures of Childhood; Books, Toys and Games from the Opie Collection.* Arcade Publishing, 1989.

Pellowski, Anne. *The World of Storytelling.* H. W. Wilson Co., 1990.

Publisher's Weekly, Advertisements or announcements in the following issues: Nov. 24, 1906, p. 218; Nov. 30, 1907, p. 58; Nov. 28, 1908, p. 53; Nov. 27, 1909, p. 60; Nov. 21, 1914, p. 74; Sept. 22, 1928, p. 965; Aug. 30, 1930, p. 810; Aug. 26, 1939, p. 689; Aug. 30, 1947.

The Renier Collection of Historic and Contemporary Children's Books. Occasional Lists, No. 1-7, 1987-1990. Compiled by Tessa Chester. Bethnal Green Museum of Childhood, London, England.

Sotheby, London. Book and Manuscript Department. Auction Catalogs. Among the catalogs that include sales of cloth children's books are these: *Children's Books and Juvenilia, 27 February 1967; A Highly Important Collection of Children's Books, 21-22 October 1974; Children's Books and Juvenilia 23-24 May 1983; Children's Books, Juvenilia and Related Drawings 21-22 November 1983.*

Whalley, Joyce I. and Tessa R. Chester. *A History of Children's Book Illustration.* Godine, 1990.

Bibliography related to books for special children

Bellander, Elsie and Beata Lundstrom. *How to Publish Easy Reader Books—a Model*. Stockholm: Skoloverstyrelsen, 1987. 41 p. ISBN 91-7662-365-3

Books for Disabled Young People; an Annotated Bibliography. IBBY Documentation Centre of Books for Disabled Young People, Norwegian Institute for Special Education. Order from IBBY Secretariat, Nonnenweg 12, CH 4003 Basel, Switzerland. ISBN 82-90363-34-6

Books for Language-retarded Children. Paris, UNESCO, 1985. 114 p. (No. 20 in the series Studies on Books and Reading)

Greene, Laura and Eva Barash Dicker. *Sign Language Talk*. New York, Franklin Watts, 1989. 95 p. ISBN 0-531-10597-0

Orjasaeter, Tordis. *The Role of Children's Books in Integrating Handicapped Children into Everyday Life*. Paris, UNESCO, 1981. (No. 1 in the series Studies on Books and Reading)

Seminar Easy to Read: Papers, Criteria, Results. Dutch Centre for Public Libraries and Literature, The Hague, The Netherlands, 1989. 104 p. ISBN 90-6252-119-3

Some useful how-to-draw books

Brookes, Mona. *Drawing with Children/A Creative Teaching and Learning Method That Works for Adults, Too*. Jeremy P. Tarcher, Inc., 1986.

Edwards, Betty. *Drawing on the Right Side of the Brain*. Jeremy P. Tarcher, Inc., 1991 revised.

Emberley, Ed. *Ed Emberley's Big Green Drawing Book*. Little Brown, 1979.

O'Neill, Dan. *The Big Yellow Drawing Book*. Hugh O'Neill and Associates, 1974.

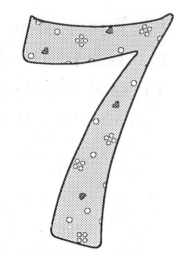

Resources

Marla Ostrowski's version of a "quiet" or "busy" book uses sewing techniques throughout, including the simple texts, in cursive writing worked with a satin stitch on the sewing machine.

Patterns for cloth books

Many of these patterns are out of print and are generally not available from commercial outlets. They can occasionally be found through out-of-print pattern sources.

"Country Countdown." Butterick Pattern 4837. Pattern for a counting book from 1 to 10, depicting animals on a farm.

"How to Sew a Quiet Book" adapted from a book submitted by Annella Simmons. Craft Course Publishers, 1977. Re-issued,1981.

"It's a Zoo. Children's Book & Appliqué Transfers." Vogue Pattern 1959. Includes heat set transfers for numbers, alphabet, and six animal characters. The finished book allows the child to learn tying shoelaces and bows, buttoning, buckling and braiding.

"My First Book." Directions for making a simple cloth book, suggested by Pat Pardo, George Bruce Branch, New York Public Library. In: *Patterns for Pre-Schoolers; Programs and Services in Public Libraries.* Youth Services Section, New York Library Association, 1985.

"My Muppet Book." Vogue Pattern 8902. © Henson Associates,1984. Patterns for making a book using many of the puppet characters created by Jim Henson for Sesame Street.

"One, Two, See What I Can Do." Butterick Pattern 5626. Instructions for making a book or frieze with 5 panels. Activities include matching colors, weaving a basket, buttoning.

Andres, Lenore and Pat Van Nes. "Quiet Time Book." In *The Mother's Book: Practical Ideas for Parenting.* Fortress Press, 1988. ISBN 0-919797-56-3. This includes patterns for a book intended to keep children occupied while in church or Sunday school, with such activities as zipping, buttoning, tying, closing snaps.

Sage, Janet. *Busy Christians. Patterns for Cloth Books* and *Busy Bible 1,2,3. Patterns for Cloth Books.* Concordia, 1978. These are exactly what the titles suggest—

patterns for making religious books for children. Each of them involves activities such as lifting flaps, buttoning buttons, zipping zippers, etc. They are intended for young children, to keep them occupied during religious services, or during Sunday School sessions.

Books about making books

Evans, Joy and Jo Ellen Moore. *How to Make Books with Children* and *How to Make Big Books with Children.* Evan-Moore Publications. ISBN 1-55799-061-1

These are actually meant for the teacher to use in the classroom, with paper and cardboard. However, a number of the ideas and patterns would translate quite well to cloth. These manuals are especially helpful to the person looking for ideas on how to handle pop-up or flap-lifting elements on a page.

Irvine, Joan illus. by Barbara Reid. *How to Make Pop-Ups.* Kids Can Press, Morrow, 1987. ISBN 0-688-07902-4 (paper)

The author has worked with many groups to create paper pop-up books. Many of her clever ideas can transfer to cloth.

McCormick, Christine E. and Jana M. Mason. *Little Books.* Scott Foresman, 1990. (Good Year Books). ISBN 0-673-38878-6

This is intended for the early childhood teacher. However, it has many simple, clever and attractive ideas that could stimulate any individual making a book for a young child.

Fashions from Memories; How to Transfer Photo Copies & More to Fabric. Picture This, Plaid Enterprises, 1649 International Blvd., P. O. Box 7600, Norcross, Ga. 30091.

Although this gives instructions and materials for transfering photos to clothing, many of the ideas would work on cloth books as well.

Hiner, Mark. *Paper Engineering for Pop-up Books and Cards.* Tarquin Publishers, 1985.

This is similar to the first two books listed in this section, but with even more elaborate directions. Some of the ideas would transfer well to cloth books.

In the image: "and the big elephant!" / "On the way home Joey stopped at" / "Grandma's house in Cleveland. In her garden he saw two white e.. poking up through the lettuce pl.." / "what animal is hiding there?"

Fig. 7-1. Children love the textures in this book.

Shulevitz, Uri. *Writing with Pictures: How to Write and Illustrate Children's Books.* Watson-Guptill, 1985. ISBN 0-8230-5940-5

One of the best guides ever published for persons seriously interested in pursuing their creative talents in writing and/or illustrating for children. This guide is also excellent for showing the average parent or teacher some of the things to look for when evaluating the artistry hidden behind the actual pages of children's books.

Melton, David. *Written and Illustrated by...; a revolutionary two-brain approach for teaching students how to write and illustrate amazing books.* Landmark Editions, 1988. ISBN 0-933849-00-1.

As the sub-title suggests, this is really intended for the classroom teacher, and emphasizes how book-making projects can be incorporated into the language arts curriculum. However, non-teachers might get some ideas that could transfer to cloth book-making projects.

Persons who make cloth books to order

These individuals have indicated they make cloth books on special order. In many cases, the books can be personalized for a specific child/children in a specific family or place. Prices tend to range from $60 to $100 per book, depending upon the complexity. When writing them for a listing of what they offer, please send a stamped, self-addressed envelope.

Marla Ostrowski
396 West Mulberry St.
Kankakee, Illinois 60901

Julie Krackow
c/o Center for Making Cloth Books
830 West Wabasha
Winona, Minnesota 55987

Fig. 7-2. *Two examples of handmade cloth books that are sold commercially. On the left is one of the many titles available through Lillian Vernon. On the right is the ABC book available through Pockets of Learning.*

Commercially available cloth books

The following titles were available as of January 1992. Prices, if given, are as listed in 1991 catalogs; check with the supplier for the current price and availability of each item.

ABC Book. Produced by Pockets of Learning. Can be ordered from The Right Start Catalog, 5334 Sterling Center Drive, Westlake Village, Ca. 91361. $39.95.

Baby's First Cloth Books: Titles include *Baby Animals* ISBN 0-79808-84244-0, *Baby's First Picture Book* ISBN 0-79808-84245-7, *The Cow Says Moo* ISBN 0-79808-841313. Random House Publishers.

Cuddle Cloth Books: Titles include *Baby Animals Say Hello* ISBN 0-79808-88241-5;

Baby's Cradle Songs ISBN 0-79808-88242-2; *Baby's Favorite Things* ISBN 0-79808-87470-0 and others. Random House Publishers.

Cuddle Doll Books: Little Rabbit's Garden ISBN 0-79808-87112-x. Random House Publishers, $3.95.

My Busy Book, 381397; *More Busy Book Fun,* 381497; *My Counting Book,* 375797; *My Bedtime Book,* 411797. Produced in China and distributed by Lillian Vernon, Mount Vernon, NY. $14.98 ea.

The Pocket Book. Designed, produced and distributed by Sas Colby and Design Matters, 138 Crofton, San Antonio, Tx. 78210. $45.00

An adaptation of the "Quiet Book" idea, only in this case all of the opening, zipping, buttoning, and buckling is related to pockets.

Soft Chunky Books: Titles include *Baby at Home* ISBN 0-79808-81924-4; *Baby in the Park* ISBN 0-79808-81925-1. Random House Publishers.

Mail-order supply list

Aardvark Adventures
Box 2449
Livermore, CA 94550
Squeakers, threads, interesting doo-dads, funny newsletter for customers. Catalog, $1.

Baer Fabrics
515 E Market St
Louisville, KY 40202
Comprehensive stock of fabrics. Catalog, $2.

Britex-by-Mail
146 Geary
San Francisco, CA 94108
All kinds of fabric. Send long pre-addressed stamped envelope.

Cabin Fever Calicos
PO Box 550106
Atlanta, GA 30355
Quilt books, fabrics, etc.

Clotilde, Inc.
1909 SW First Ave
Ft. Lauderdale, FL 33315
Fusible interfacings, threads, notions. Catalog, $1.

Donna Salyers' Fabulous Furs
700 Madison Ave.
Covington, KY 41011
Fur scraps.

G Street Fabrics
11854 Rockville Pike
Rockville, MD 20852
Any fabric available by mail. $2 swatch service.

Herrschners, Inc.
Hoover Rd
Stevens Point, WI 54492
Supplies for all needlearts.

Keepsake Quilting
PO Box 1459
Meredith, NH 03253
Books, notions, quilting supplies.

Nancy's Notions
PO Box 683
Beaver Dam, WI 53916
Fusible interfacings, threads, notions.

National Thread & Supply
695 Red Oak Rd
Stockbridge, GA 30281
Sewing supplies and thread.

Newark Dressmaker Supply
Box 2448Lehigh Valley, PA 18001
Sewing supplies.

Saks Arts & Crafts
2405 S Calhoun Rd
New Berlin, WI 53151
(800) 558-6696
Comprehensive crafts supply. Catalog, $4.

Sew Art International
PO Box 550
Bountiful, UT 84010
Unusual sewing threads.

Sew/Fit Co
PO Box 565
LaGrange, IL 60525
Sewing notions and accessories.

Speed Stitch
3113 Broadpoint Dr
Harbor Heights, FL 33983
Sulky rayon threads and machine-embroidery supplies. Catalog, $3 (refundable with order).

Solar-Kist Corp.
PO Box 273
La Grange, IL 60525
Teflon sheet, Fine Fuse fusible web.

Treadleart
25834-I Narbonne Ave
Lomita, CA 90717
Fusible interfacings, threads, machine-embroidery supplies.

Ultrascraps
PO Box 96
Farmington, UT 84025
Ultrasuede scraps. Catalog, $1.

Zoodads
PO Box 15073
Riverside, RI 02915
Wonderful print fabrics.

Index

89

Index

Literacy groups

Barbara Bush Foundation for Family Literacy
1002 Wisconsin Ave NW
Washington, DC 20007
(202) 338-2006

Coalition for Literacy
Contact Center
P.O. Box 81826
Lincoln, NE 68501
(800) 228-8813

Literacy Pass It On Campaign
(Coors Literacy Hotline)
311-10th St
Golden, CO 80401
(800) 626-4601

Laubach Literacy Action
1320 Jamesville Ave, Box 131
Syracuse, NY 13210
(315) 422-9121

Literacy Volunteers of America
5795 Widewaters Parkway
Syracuse, NY 13214
(315) 445-8000

Reading is Fundamental
600 Maryland Ave SW, Suite 500
Washington, DC 20024
(202) 287-3220

Additional copies of *How to Make Cloth Books for Children* can be ordered from Open Chain Publishing, Inc., PO Box 2634-B, Menlo Park, CA 94026: $17.50 ($18.75 California residents).

Wholesale orders are welcome. Please contact Chilton Book Company, Radnor, PA 19089, (800) 695-1214.